Vice & Virtue
The Battle Within

Vice & Virtue

The Battle Within

JIM DIXON

Grace Blvd. Publishing

Vice & Virtue: The Battle Within
Copyright © 2001 by Dr. James S. Dixon

Printed by Johnson's Printing, Boulder, Colorado

For information contact:
    Cherry Hills Community Church/Grace Blvd. Publishing
    3900 E. Grace Boulevard
    Highlands Ranch, Colorado 80126
    303-791-4100
    www.chcc.org

ISBN: 0-9709186-0-7

CONTENTS

Acknowledgments vii

Introduction ix

Vice

ONE: Pride 3

TWO: Greed 13

THREE: Lust 25

FOUR: Envy 35

FIVE: Gluttony 45

SIX: Sloth 55

SEVEN: Anger 65

Virtue

EIGHT: Faith 77

NINE: Hope 87

TEN: Love 97

ELEVEN: Justice 109

TWELVE: Wisdom 123

THIRTEEN: Self-Control 131

FOURTEEN: Courage 139

FIFTEEN: Humility 149

ACKNOWLEDGMENTS

Many people have made this book possible.

My special gratitude to the group of men who financed and encouraged this work: Paul Lewan, Lloyd Lewan, John Benson, Jerre Dixon, Greg Dixon, Tim Scates, Everett Dye, Norm Jensen, Bill Nelson, Sam Searcy, Bill Pauls, Bill Bostrom, and Dutch Franz. These men have had the grace and mercy to believe in the ministry God has entrusted to me. My special thanks to Dutch Franz, my co-worker and friend, who organized this group.

I thank Steve Sorenson and Kathy Passerine for adapting and editing this work.

My heartfelt thanks to Lorna Kissinger who faithfully transcribes my sermons each week.

My gratitude is greatest to Barbara, my wife, who oversaw this project. She is my best and eternal friend.

I will always be grateful to the elders, staff, and congregation of Cherry Hills Community Church where I have been blessed to serve.

INTRODUCTION

The war between good and evil began in heaven (Revelation 12) and extended to Eden (Genesis 3). This conflict has been portrayed in literature, from Golding's *Lord of the Flies* to Tolkien's *Lord of the Rings*. This battle will continue until Armageddon and will conclude at the return of Christ and the Last Judgment.

Today the battle is waging within the life of every Christian. It is a struggle for sanctification and for the very character of Christ. In this struggle each believer has the potent help of the indwelling Holy Spirit. It is my prayer that God's Spirit will use this book in your life as you struggle "against the world rulers of this present darkness" (Ephesians 6:12).

The monastic community under the influence of Gregory the Great identified the seven deadly sins as pride, greed, lust, envy, gluttony, sloth, and anger. They are considered deadly, not in the sense that they are mortal or beyond pardon but rather in the sense that they are capital or root sins. They most likely lead to other sins.

The seven cardinal virtues as enunciated by the medieval church are faith, hope, love, justice, wisdom, self-control, and courage. The first three are considered theological and represent the Pauline triad in 1 Corinthians 13:13. The other four are considered natural or moral virtues and originated in the philosophical thought of ancient Greece. Augustine reinterpreted these virtues from a Christian and biblical perspective and viewed them as essential to the Christian's proper devotion to God. I have taken the liberty of adding a chapter on humility to the seven chapters on virtues because humility, I firmly believe, is a core virtue in the Christian's life.

Vice

P*ride*

CHAPTER ONE

When you think of people who have made great discoveries, whose names come to mind? Galileo? Leonardo da Vinci? Cyrus McCormick? Henry Ford?

The names that come to my mind are Donald Schneider, James Gunn, and Maarten Schmidt. Perhaps you haven't heard of these three scientists. They didn't walk on the moon, explore the deck of the sunken Titanic, or receive a Nobel prize. They discovered a new quasar on the very edge of our known universe.

A quasar is an irregular galaxy one hundred to one thousand times more luminous than a normal galaxy. Being the most distant object discovered in space, this particular quasar is one hundred times brighter than the Milky Way Galaxy in which we live. It's also a mind-boggling distance away. Traveling at 186,000 miles per second, the light emanating from this distant quasar takes more than ten billion years to travel to Earth.

What's really startling, however, is that scientists believe that more than one hundred billion galaxies exist in our universe. Obviously, that means Earth is incredibly small in comparison to other planets and even less significant when compared to the number of planets in other galaxies. That also means we humans could be viewed as mere specks on this small, rotating ball called Earth in a remote part of the cosmos.

How does that make you feel? Most people don't like to feel like mere specks. They want to view themselves as being at the center of their universe, as being quite important.

This unfolding information about the universe communicates a great truth about God, the Creator who loves each of us. Thousands of years ago David recognized the greatness of God in the context of the universe:

> When I consider your heavens, the work of your fingers, the moon and the stars, which you have set in place, what is man that you are mindful of him, the son of man that you care for him? . . . The heavens declare the glory of God; the skies proclaim the work of his hands.
>
> Psalm 8:3-4, 19:1

As seen in Romans 1:20, the apostle Paul recognized the extent to which God's character has been revealed through the created universe:

> For since the creation of the world, God's invisible qualities — His eternal power and divine nature — have been clearly seen, being understood from what has been made, so that men are without excuse.

Adam and Eve lived amidst the perfection of Eden and clearly saw God's character revealed. But were they content to allow God to remain at the center of their universe? No. They wanted to be like God. They chose, like people who followed after them, to worship created things rather than to worship the Creator (Romans 1:25).

What is the word to describe this rebellion and self-glorification? It is sinful pride, an incomprehensibly inflated view of self. Proud people become the center of their own universe, even when they are dwarfed by God and His creation.

The Origin of Pride

Pride, the Bible records in Ezekiel 28:12,15-17, originated with Satan, the fallen angel:

> You were the model of perfection, full of wisdom and perfect in beauty. . . . You were blameless in your ways from the day you were created till wickedness was found in you. Through your widespread trade you were filled with violence, and you sinned. So I drove you in disgrace from the mount of God, and I expelled you, O guardian cherub, from among the fiery stones. Your heart became proud on account of your beauty, and you corrupted your wisdom because of your splendor. So I threw you to the earth; I made a spectacle of you before kings.

The words in Isaiah 14:12-15 echo Satan's fall:

> How you have fallen from heaven, O morning star, son of the dawn! You have been cast down to the earth, you who once laid low the nations! You said in your heart, 'I will ascend to heaven; I will raise my throne above the stars of God; I will sit enthroned on the mount of assembly, on the utmost heights of the sacred mountain. I will ascend above the tops of the clouds; I will make myself like the Most High.' But you are brought down to the grave, to the depths of the pit.

Satan corrupted his wisdom for the sake of splendor. He said in his heart, "I will ascend above the tops of the clouds; I will make myself like the Most High." What was the result? God cast him out of heaven as a profane being.

The Subtlety of *Ubris*

Perhaps you are thinking: *That's true of Satan, but that's not true of me. I don't want to ascend above the stars. I don't want to establish my throne on high. I don't want to make myself like God, to put myself above Him.* Unfortunately, pride is subtle. It creeps into our lives in insidious ways.

Have you heard of the Pillars of Hercules? These two giant rock formations stand on either side of the Strait of Gibraltar (located at the eastern end of the mouth of the Mediterranean Sea where it enters the North Atlantic Ocean). Today these formations are called the Rock of Gibraltar and Mt. Acho, but during ancient times they were called Calpe and Abyla.

Ancient people believed that the gods didn't want anyone to travel beyond the Strait of Gibraltar, beyond the Pillars of Hercules. They drew paintings and minted coins portraying the Pillars of Hercules and an endless sea that contained these words: *ne plus altra*, meaning "no more beyond." To travel beyond that point, they believed, violated the will of the gods.

If any sailor traveled beyond the Pillars of Hercules, the Greeks called that action *ubris*. That's the predominant Greek word translated pride today! You see, the Greeks believed that the essence of pride was to go beyond the boundaries of the gods. That act required arrogance and insolence.

Today you and I are tempted to venture beyond the boundaries that God has established for us. Just as Adam and Eve ventured past God's laws and boundaries, we are drawn to do the same. When we place our will above His will and our wants above His wants, we exhibit pride; and that's sin.

God knows our hearts, the core of our being. (See Acts 1:24; Psalm 139:23; Psalm 44:20-21.) He knows that our hearts are deceitfully wicked (Jeremiah 17:9). He defines sin as the thoughts we think and the actions we do that break His boundaries.

Chapter One: Pride

Who Is Really Great?

Have you asked yourself recently, *What am I living for?* Although it can seem intimidating, this question is extremely relevant. Are you living to serve yourself? Honor yourself? Please yourself? Are your goals centered on yourself? If so, in the sight of God, you have pridefully placed yourself above Him and are living beyond His boundaries.

Is Christ at the center of your life? Is pursuing His kingdom your highest purpose? How are you using your money, talents, abilities, and time? They reflect who is most important in your life—you or God.

Consider Louis XIV, the King of France from 1643-1715. He was, you may remember, called by such names as "Grand Monarch," "The Sun King," and "Louis the Great." He ruled France for seventy-two years, longer than any other modern European monarch.

If you've seen photographs or visited the incomparable Palace of Versailles, you've also seen the work of Louis XIV. He had the palace built. In order to do that, however, he drained the national treasuries and taxed most French people into poverty. In fact, he lived in opulent splendor while many French peasants starved. When someone (who may have lost his head on a guillotine) told Louis XIV to subject himself to the State, Louis XIV indignantly snapped, "I am the State."

When the king died, his body was wrapped in royal clothing. The Bishop of France gave one of the greatest eulogies ever. He didn't focus on details of the palace. He didn't mention the suffering French people. He didn't even mention the transition of power and the hopes of a better future for the country. No. He spoke just four words. The bishop looked at the body of Louis XIV, looked back at the people, and stated, "God alone is great." Then the bishop sat down.

If you really believe that God alone is great, you won't allow pride to develop in your heart. You will humble yourself before God. You will place Him at the center of your life. You will live to further His kingdom and not your own. You will never set yourself above Him.

The Trap of Snobbery

During the 1500's and 1600's, only the nobility were permitted to attend a college or a university in England. The common people, considered lower-class servants, were excluded. In time Oxford University administrators decided to allow the common people to attend the university on one condition. Freshmen commoners had to complete a form upon their arrival that identified their social status as being *sine nobilitate* — without nobility.

As time passed, according to some sources, the common people abbreviated those words. College and university students who lacked nobility became labeled *snobs*. More time passed, and the word *snob* came to describe anyone pretending to be nobility who looked down on other people. Ultimately, the word *snob* has come to refer to anyone who looks down on others.

Do you want to be known for being snobbish? I certainly don't, and I'm sure you don't either. Yet if you and I have pride in our hearts, we are indeed snobs! We have placed ourselves above other people.

Do you remember the parable of the two men who went into the temple to pray? Recorded in Luke 18:10-13, Jesus told this parable to people who were looking down on other people.

> Two men went up to the temple to pray, one a Pharisee and the other a tax collector. The Pharisee stood up and prayed about himself: 'God, I thank you that I am not like other men — robbers, evildoers, adulterers — or even like this tax collector. I fast twice a week and give a tenth of all I get.'

> But the tax collector stood at a distance. He would not even look up to heaven, but beat his breast and said, 'God, have mercy on me, a sinner.'

The Pharisee's statement is really amazing, not just because of the words in his prayer but because of the comparison he chose to make. He could have compared himself to prophets, priests, or kings; but he didn't. Pride isn't like that. In addition to setting himself above God, this proud Pharisee chose to compare himself to someone he viewed as being beneath him — in this case the tax collector, whom society hated. In effect, the Pharisee said, "God, thank you that I'm not like this poor slob. I'm above him."

In verse 14, Jesus revealed the consequences of both men's responses.

> I tell you that this man [the tax collector], rather than the other [the Pharisee], went home justified before God. For everyone who exalts himself will be humbled, and he who humbles himself will be exalted.

Do you really want to humble yourself before God and before other people, or do you want to exalt yourself?

What's Our Deeper Motivation?

Recently, I read about the United States election of 1872. Ulysses S. Grant was the incumbent Republican President. He was not considered to be a viable candidate for re-election because his administration had been corrupt and he had been accused of alcoholism.

Confident they'd win, the liberal republicans and democrats nominated Horace Greeley, the editor of the *New York Tribune*. (Greeley had popularized the famous statement, "Go west, young man, go west," first used by an Indiana newspaperman in 1851.) A brilliant journalist, Horace wasn't much of a politician; and the nation complained about his qualifications. In fact, he became a tragic political figure who maintained excessively liberal views. He advocated communal living and tried to establish social-economic communities that practiced socialism. He established a cooperative community in Colorado and called it Union Colony. Today the city of Greeley is named after him.

That same year a multi-millionaire named George Francis Train also ran for the United States presidency. His claim to fame was that he had traveled around the world faster than any other man had. (In fact, Jules Verne wrote *Around the Word in Eighty Days* based on Train's life.) But Train seemed to fall into trouble everywhere he went and had the dubious distinction of being imprisoned in more than fifteen countries during his travels. What was Train's goal? He no longer wanted to travel around the world. He wanted to rule the world. He gave over a thousand speeches to more than two million people. Incredibly, he even charged admission to his presidential speeches. Today he is said to be the only man who made money running for the United States presidency!

What motivated such a strange trio of people to seek our nation's highest office? Did they really want to serve other people? Did they really believe they were the best qualified candidates? Only God knows, but psychologists reveal that many people seek positions of leadership and authority not because they want to serve or because they believe themselves to be qualified but because they want prominence. They desire to be exalted, to ascend above other people. People have always responded pridefully. Pride creeps into the workplace, the home, friendships, and the real motivation for being kind.

A Look at Jesus' Teaching

Two thousand years ago in Israel, the head of a household would commonly invite guests and friends to share a special meal on the Sabbath. If he was powerful and a member of the ruling class, he customarily invited well-known or even controversial people to the gathering.

The principal piece of furniture used during the Sabbath meal was a triclinium, a kind of couch that held three people. During a Sabbath meal, these couches were always arranged in a "U" shape. The one who sat in the triclinium in the middle of the base of the "U" was granted the highest honor. The person to this guest-of-honor's left received the next level of exaltation. The person to this guest-of-honor's right was considered to be the third-ranking person. The level of honor decreased as people sat farther away from the couch of honor.

For some reason a member of the Sanhedrin, the prominent religious council of that day, invited Jesus to a Sabbath meal. Intensely scrutinized by the Pharisees and experts of the Jewish law, Jesus challenged them by asking, "Is it lawful to heal on the Sabbath or not?" Receiving no reply, Jesus healed a man and sent him away.

But Jesus wasn't finished dealing with the proud hearts of the religious leaders. His momentum was building; the timing was right. Noticing how various guests picked places of honor, he told a parable.

> When someone invites you to a wedding feast, do not take the place of honor, for a person more distinguished than you may have been invited. If so, the host who invited both of you will come and say to you, 'Give this man your seat.' Then, humiliated, you will have to take the least important place.

> But when you are invited, take the lowest place, so that when your host comes, he will say to you, 'Friend, move up to a better place.' Then you will be honored in the presence of all your fellow guests. For everyone who exalts himself will be humbled, and he who humbles himself will be exalted.
>
> Luke 14:8-11

Jesus strongly condemned pride, not only with His words but with His actions. He came not to be served but to serve. He gave His life as a ransom for many. He calls us to humble ourselves as well. Pride is a sin. One day proud people will be humbled.

Clearly, the teaching of Jesus Christ is antithetical to the usual teaching of the world. Whose teaching do you really want to live by? Do you want to serve and to be Christlike? Do you want to honor and to exalt other people in Christlike ways? If you have achieved a position of prominence, will you view others as Jesus did with a desire to serve them?

How easy it is, even as Christians, to place ourselves above God and people. God wants us to strive for a higher calling. He wants us to elevate others and not ourselves. He wants us to put Him on the throne of our lives and to remain within His boundaries.

Greed

CHAPTER TWO

On June 14, 1968, a photograph of David Kennedy appeared in *Life* magazine. About five or six years old, he is sitting on the White House lawn looking over the property. Jacqueline Kennedy, David's aunt, had taken the photograph years earlier. John F. Kennedy, his uncle, had signed it and written, "A future president examines his property."

David had the Kennedy name. He possessed Kennedy status and wealth. He had virtually everything money could buy. But he never became a United States President, for on April 26, 1984, at the age of twenty-eight, he died of a drug overdose.

Magazines and newspapers publish articles and photographs of the rich and famous. Later these publications mourn the deaths of these same individuals who have, for example, lost their lives because of accidental overdoses or drunken mishaps. In search of the perfect relationship, tycoons treat marriage like business deals, divorcing and remarrying numerous times. Young people who have earned millions of dollars in computer companies can't spend their money fast enough. They own multiple cars, jets, twelve-thousand-square-foot houses located on beautiful beaches, and other so-called status symbols. But are these people satisfied because of their wealth and status?

Although money is a helpful resource, it cannot satisfy the deepest longings people have. It cannot provide purpose, fulfillment, or joy. Although some people have finally realized this truth (even though they'd be surprised to learn that it is straight from the Bible), many other people are consumed with the desire to pursue and to obtain more and more. Some will use virtually any means necessary to obtain it. The Bible calls this consuming desire for more money *greed*.

Two words used in the Bible are translated greed. *Philarguros* means "the love of money," and *pleonexia* means "to want more." Thus a greedy person loves money and always wants more of it. Ecclesiastes 5:10 states, "Whoever loves money never has money enough; whoever loves wealth is never satisfied with his income. This too is meaningless." Paul wrote, "For the love of money is a root of all kinds of evil" (1 Timothy 6:10). Greed is deadly.

Greed Destroys Physical and Spiritual Life

Years ago the hides of raccoons were worth quite a bit of money, so trappers set traps and snares in order to catch these animals. One trap was constructed in the shape of a box. On one side of the box were bars spaced just far enough apart to allow a raccoon's paw to reach inside.

To set the trap, the trapper would place it in a promising location and hang tinfoil inside. A passing raccoon would be attracted to the glitter of the tinfoil, venture over to the box, reach inside, and grab the tinfoil. With the tinfoil securely in his paw, the raccoon, unfortunately, couldn't remove his paw without dropping his prized possession. If the racoon was still clinging to the tinfoil when the trapper returned hours later, the trapper could easily take the animal's life.

In a similar fashion, greed is a trap that Satan uses to ensnare us; and because of its destructive nature, the Bible strongly condemns it.

> But among you, there must not be even a hint of
> sexual immorality, or of any kind of impurity, or of
> greed, because these are improper for God's holy

people. . . . For of this you can be sure: No immoral, impure or greedy person — such a man is an idolater — has any inheritance in the kingdom of Christ and of God.

Ephesians 5:3,5

People who want to get rich, fall into temptation and a trap and into many foolish and harmful desires that plunge men into ruin and destruction.

1 Timothy 6:9

For from within, out of men's hearts, come evil thoughts, sexual immorality, theft, murder, adultery, [and] greed . . . . Watch out! Be on your guard against all kinds of greed; a man's life does not consist in the abundance of his possessions.

Mark 7:21-22 and Luke 12:15

Do not wear yourself out to get rich; have the wisdom to show restraint. Cast but a glance at riches, and they are gone, for they will surely sprout wings and fly off to the sky like an eagle.

Proverbs 23:4-5

Sometimes greed literally leads to people's physical destruction as some inhabitants of Pompeii, Italy, discovered 1,919 years ago. Living in the resort capital of the Greek and Roman world, rich and famous people built second and third homes overlooking the Mediterranean Sea. Pompeii's mild and sunny climate, combined with its beautiful scenery, created an idyllic location for relaxation and business. But on August 24 in 79 A.D., Mt. Vesuvius erupted and spewed volcanic ash, cinders, and poisonous fumes over the city. Within a short time the entire city was buried.

Vice & Virtue: The Battle Within

Eager to discover what had so quickly been buried, archaeologists began excavating Pompeii in 1748. Learning that about eighteen thousand of the city's approximately twenty thousand inhabitants had been able to escape, they wondered why the other two thousand people had not. They found the bodies of those who died perfectly preserved in the ash. Clenching precious golden objects, many were found trapped in their beautiful homes. The archaeologists concluded that these people must have believed that the devastation would pass them by. Perhaps others returned to the city to retrieve prized possessions and were unable to escape again.

So what does this have to do with me? you may be thinking. *I'm not afraid that greed is literally going to lead to my physical death.*

God wants us to understand that the real danger of greed is that it will take our spiritual lives. Consider the following passages:

> No one can serve two masters. Either he will hate the one and love the other, or he will be devoted to the one and despise the other. You cannot serve both God and Money. . . . What good will it be for a man if he gains the whole world, yet forfeits his soul? Or what can a man give in exchange for his soul?
>
> Matthew 6:24 and 16:26

> Some people, eager for money, have wandered from the faith and pierced themselves with many griefs.
>
> 1 Timothy 6:10

> Do not love the world or anything in the world. If anyone loves the world, the love of the Father is not in him.
>
> 1 John 2:15

Now listen, you rich people, weep and wail because
of the misery that is coming upon you. Your wealth
has rotted, and moths have eaten your clothes. Your
gold and silver are corroded. Their corrosion will
testify against you and eat your flesh like fire. You
have hoarded wealth in the last days.

James 5:1-3

Greed literally sucks the spiritual life from our bodies. God has
created us in such a way that when we live for the accumulation of
money and the things that money can buy, we lose spiritual life in the
process.

Consider the story of the rich man (Luke 18:18-25) who asked
Jesus, "Good teacher, what must I do to inherit eternal life?"

Jesus answered, "Sell everything you have and give to the poor,
and you will have treasure in heaven. Then come, follow me."

Did the man follow Jesus? No. He went away sadly, unwilling
to give away his wealth. Jesus knew that the ruler loved money and that
he'd never experience spiritual life until he was willing to let go of his
riches.

The late Mother Teresa said, "We'll never know that Jesus is all
we need until Jesus is all we have." It's strange, but true, that often we
have to lose physical possessions before we begin to discover spiritual
life as God intends it to be. Greed destroys spiritual life.

Greed Destroys Relationships

Jesus told the rich ruler to sell everything he had and to give it
to the poor. Why? Greed does more than destroy the lives of greedy
people. It destroys the lives of those people who need what the greedy
people are hoarding.

God does not tell each of us to sell everything, but He does tell
all of us to remember the poor. We have a certain obligation to our
neighbors and to other people who are less fortunate than we are.

Defend the cause of the weak and fatherless; maintain
the rights of the poor and oppressed. Rescue the weak
and needy.

Psalm 82:3-4

He who despises his neighbor sins, but blessed is he
who is kind to the needy.

Proverbs 14:21

When you give a luncheon or dinner, do not invite
your friends, your brothers or relatives, or your rich
neighbors; if you do, they may invite you back and
so you will be repaid. But when you give a banquet,
invite the poor, the crippled, the lame, the blind, and
you will be blessed. Although they cannot repay you,
you will be repaid at the resurrection of the righteous.

Luke 14:12-14

When people do not share with poor people, poor people die.
More than one billion people in the world are starving. Tonight more
than one billion people will go to bed hungry. Forty thousand people
will starve to death today and tomorrow and the next day! In most cases
this is not because these people are lazy; it's because other people have
chosen not to love, give, or share their wealth.

Is this just a statistic to you? What do you feel when you read
this? If you could watch each of those forty thousand people die, I know
that you'd be deeply moved. God sees each of them, and He is deeply
moved.

We in the United States live in a prosperous nation. We are so
prosperous, in fact, that we have between twenty-nine and thirty-five
million dogs and as many as fifty-five million cats as household pets!
We spend billions of dollars every year to feed them, and veterinarians
reveal that many of our pets are obese. Am I anti-dog and anti-cat? No.

Chapter Two: Greed

My family has two well-fed dogs, and we love them. But I sometimes wonder how God feels when He sees us spending billions of dollars on our pets while so many people are starving to death.

The Bible tells us that throughout the ages a great conflict has existed between good and evil. In the Book of Revelation, we read that during the end times, at the consummation of the age, this great conflict will increase. Polarization will occur. Many different names are given to the forces of evil on the earth, including Babylon (Revelation 17-18). Babylon, the great whore, will be an earthly power that trades with the nations of the world, consumes most of the world's goods, and entices the world to commit immorality.

During the 1930's and 1940's, many people believed that Nazi Germany was the end times Babylon. During the 1950's, 1960's, and even into the 1970's, many people identified the Soviet Union and Communism with Babylon. Today, however, many evangelical Christians around the world — particularly those in the Third World — consider the United States to be the end times Babylon because the United States exhibits so much greed, individually and corporately.

The concept of the end times Babylon in the Bible is complex and cannot really be identified with any nation. Certainly, the United States has helped people all over the world many times and in many different ways, but God would remind Americans today that

> from everyone who has been given much, much will be demanded; and from the one who has been entrusted with much, much more will be asked.
>
> Luke 12:48b

Greed kills, not just internationally but ecclesiastically. Greed will destroy our churches if we allow it to do so. Each of us must strive to make the church we attend a giving church — one that supports needy people in the name of Jesus Christ. In what ways is your church a giving church? Maybe your church supports a Christian organization that helps children and families who live in the Third World. Maybe your church has a food bank that distributes food to hungry people in your community. Maybe young people in your church hold workdays and serve older people who need help doing yardwork or cleaning their homes. Maybe your church partners with an inner-city church.

Greed also kills on an individual level. When we become greedy, we can destroy the very people we love. Remember the ancient story of Midas, king of Phrygia? He possessed great wealth, but he wanted more.

One day King Midas went to the Greek god Dionysus and asked, "Grant me one wish."

Dionysus, replied, "What is the wish?"

"Grant that whatever I touch will turn to gold," Midas responded.

"I do not want to grant you this gift," Dionysus said. "It is not a blessing. It is a curse." Yet because of the king's persistence, Dionysus finally granted his wish.

Upon leaving, the king noticed a flower in a field. He touched it. Immediately, it turned to gold. Marveling, he picked it up and thought, "What incredible value this has. What incredible wealth I have. I'm rich."

When Midas returned home, he picked up his food at the dinner table. It immediately turned to gold, and he couldn't eat. When he picked up his cup of wine, the cup turned to gold. The wine became gold as well, and he couldn't drink.

> Later in the day his little daughter, arms
> outstretched, came running to him. Panicked, Midas
> tried to ward her off; but she embraced him. Life
> flowed from her body as she turned to gold.

Many mothers and fathers today have sacrificed their children on the altar of greed. The average father, according to one study conducted by the University of Maryland, spends seven minutes a day nurturing his children. The average mother, according to that same study, spends twenty-seven minutes a day nurturing her children. What is greed's impact on the involvement parents have in their children's lives? It makes a tremendous difference.

Let's become personal for a moment. Are we consumed by our careers? Are we consumed by the pursuit of money and all that money can buy? By our example, are we teaching our children to seek that which will never satisfy? Are we allowing greed — even the most subtle forms of greed — to take away what our children need most, time with us and instruction concerning their relationship with God? Greed is insidious. It will destroy our lives and the lives of others, including those closest to us.

Greed Destroys the Church

When you think of how greed can destroy the Church, what comes to mind? Do you think of how the Roman Catholic Church exploited the masses during the Middle Ages, selling indulgences and weakening true spirituality while fattening its treasuries? Do you think of Jim Bakker and other tele-evangelists who became consumed by greed and tried to build personal empires?

Instead of focusing on the faulty leadership that sometimes exists within the institutional Church, let's focus on the greed of the laity. I suggest that the Church of Jesus Christ has little power and little ministry unless the people of Christ give of their income. The average Protestant in the United States today gives 2.7 per cent of his or her after-tax income to charitable causes and less than 2 per cent of after-tax income to the Church.

Ten, twenty, and thirty years ago, Christians gave more money to charity and to the Church. What has changed? Are people more skeptical about how churches will use donated money? Have people been soured by the small percentage of churches that have abused ministry instead of truly seeking to serve Christ? Certainly, part of the answer lies in the fact that many nominal Christians have come to Christ and maintained wrong attitudes and motives. Instead of having a desire to serve and to share, they don't want to give of their time and money.

Remember Charlemagne, whom Pope Leo III crowned Holy Roman Emperor in 800 A.D.? Considered by many to be the greatest ruler between 400 and 1500 A.D., Charlemagne reigned from 768 to 814 A.D. over most of the civilized world. He possessed great military intelligence and political genius. He was committed to Christ, but he didn't really understand the character of Christ.

You see, when he drove defeated armies into lakes and rivers, he forced the enemy soldiers to be baptized in the name of Christ so that they would become Christians. He thought he was serving Christ by doing so, but obviously he was misguided. Many of the "baptized" people rebelled, particularly the Saxons who preferred to die rather than to become baptized Christians. Realizing he needed a different approach, Charlemagne decided to use greed as an incentive. He offered fine linen wardrobes to anyone among the defeated armies who would be baptized. Suddenly, thousands of warriors volunteered to be baptized in exchange for the clothing they received.

I want to suggest that tactics today haven't changed. Millions of people still come to Christ for what they can receive: forgiveness, salvation, eternal life in heaven, God's provision and protection. Yes, God does offer these and much more to His children; but these aren't the only reasons why people should come to Jesus Christ.

A Christian isn't simply someone to whom God has made a commitment. A Christian has made a commitment to Christ. A Christian isn't simply someone to whom God has made promises. A Christian has made promises to God.

If you are truly a Christian, you have asked Jesus Christ to be your Lord. You have been born anew. You have committed your life to serve His eternal kingdom with your body, soul, and spirit. This is the essence of Christianity. This earthly life, after all, is but a drop of water in a huge bucket. The real world is yet to come.

One evening my wife Barbara and I flew from Birmingham to Denver. Upon discovering that we were returning from a missions conference, a retired man seated next to us on the airplane said, "You know, I believe in God and Jesus Christ as my Savior. But I don't often go to church, and I don't believe in giving money to churches." He paused. "Churches are always wanting money. I work hard for my money."

This sincere but misguided man doesn't understand what it really means to be a Christian. He doesn't understand what it really means to serve the Church of Jesus Christ.

What are you pursuing? To what or to whom are you committed? If you believe in your country, you will serve it when necessary. You will pay taxes and even sacrifice your life. Pulling from Oliver Wendell Holmes' speech given on May 30, 1884, John F. Kennedy said, "Ask not what your country can do for you; ask what you can do for your country." If this truth applies to earthly kingdoms, how much more should it apply to the kingdom of God? If you're a citizen of heaven, you will live in order to serve that kingdom. Sometimes that service begins with a checkbook, a pocketbook, or a wallet.

God requires, not suggests, that every Christian give a minimum of ten percent (a tithe) of his or her income to support the work of the kingdom of Christ; and if God has blessed you with financial riches, you need to give even more than a tithe.

> 'Bring the whole tithe into the storehouse, that there
> may be food in my house. Test me in this,' says the

Lord Almighty, 'and see if I will not throw open the
floodgates of heaven and pour out so much blessing
that you will not have room enough for it.'

Malachi 3:10

Sometimes people say to me, "If I'm not tithing, what should I
do? Should I volunteer more of my time? Should I increase my giving
by increments? Maybe I could give two percent next year. What do you
think about that?"

Simply, if you are not tithing, you need to repent. You need to
pray and to say, "Here I am, Lord Jesus. Use me. I want to live for the
service of your kingdom."

If the church you attend is committed to the service of God's
kingdom, it's certainly committed to reaching people with the message
of Christ. It's certainly committed to building up the laity in the name
of Christ and sending them out in His name to evangelize and to disciple
other people. If you support the vision of your church, then support it
financially.

Baseball great Yogi Berra said, "The problem with most people
in this world is they go through life with a catcher's mitt in both hands."
That statement may be true about many people in the world, but it
should never be true of Christians. God doesn't call Christians to be
simply receivers; He calls them to be givers.

Remember what Jesus said in Matthew 6:33: "Seek first his
[God's] kingdom and his righteousness, and all these things will be given
to you as well." In other words, if we seek first His kingdom, He will
give us everything we need. Instead of being greedy, we can trust Him
to provide for our needs.

$\mathcal{L}ust$

CHAPTER THREE

> Do not love the world or
> anything in the world. If anyone loves the world, the love
> of the Father is not in him. For everything in the world —
> the cravings of sinful man, the lust of his eyes and the
> boasting of what he has and does — comes not from the
> Father but from the world. The world and its desires pass
> away, but the man who does the will of God lives forever.
>
> 1 John 2:15-17

John, the apostle of our Lord Jesus Christ, wrote these inspired words about 1,900 years ago. During his day, as in ours today, wanton sexuality was rampant. The Greek word translated "lust" in this passage is *epithumia,* which primarily refers to improper sexual desire. Clearly, John was well aware of the dangers of lust as we should be today. The non-Christian inhabitants of Corinth, for example, were as lascivious as they were learned. Public prostitution comprised a key part of their religion, and the Corinthians expressed gratitude to their deities by making vows to increase the number of prostitutes.

Lust Is Sexual Desire Without Love

In 1509, at the age of eighteen, King Henry VIII ascended the throne of England. He was young, good looking, and popular. He was also gifted – able to speak many languages, a skilled musician, and a vibrant athlete. The sixteenth century was dawning, and the English people hoped that the king would usher in a golden age.

But it didn't happen. Before he died in 1547, this promising king became the laughingstock of England. His obesity became the subject of many jokes. He was so bloated as a result of gluttony that he could no longer walk. Unable to climb the stairs in his castle, he was carried in a cage lifted by a chain to the upper floors.

King Henry VIII's legacy went far beyond his obesity. He involved England in costly wars. He drained the national treasury and increased inflation. He taxed the English people into poverty. He alienated the Roman Catholic Church. He had two of his first five wives, as well as such good men as Sir Thomas More and Thomas Cromwell, executed. Why did he make such harsh decisions? What caused him to dash all the hopes of England?

Historians reveal that he became consumed by lust, and he spared no woman in pursuit of its fulfillment. After marrying his first wife, Catherine of Aragon, King Henry VIII entered into a sexual union with another woman, Mary Boleyn, several times a week. He fathered her child although he never gave the child legitimacy. Then his lustful eyes feasted on Mary's sister, Anne Boleyn, and he desired her.

"I'll not share your bed unless you share your throne," Anne Boleyn stated.

The king decided to divorce Catherine of Aragon. But the Roman Catholic Church wouldn't allow it. Therefore, he renounced the Roman Catholic Church, promoted the independence of the Church of England, and proclaimed himself the sovereign head of the Church and the State.

Following his divorce, he did marry Anne; later he had her beheaded. Other wives followed in succession: Jane Seymour, Anne of Cleves, Catherine Howard, and Catherine Parr. Did he love any of his six wives (or the hundreds of other women with whom he had affairs)? Most historians believe that he didn't have the capacity to love them. He was never faithful to any of them. Rather he used them to obtain power and pleasure. To him, women were mere objects that briefly satisfied his sexual gratification. He didn't love. He only lusted.

In contrast to biblical *agape* love that is not self-seeking (1 Corinthians 13:5), *epithumia* is self-seeking sexual desire without love. Whereas biblical love never fails (1 Corinthians 13:8), lust always ends. A person who is controlled by lust uses others (whether in reality or through the imagination), discards them after a period of time, and then looks for others.

Lust Is Sexual Desire Without Sanity

In Scripture *epithumia* always refers to excessive and exaggerated sexual desire that lacks sanity. The sexual desires of Cleopatra VII, born sixty-nine years before Jesus was born, illustrate the insanity of *epithumia*. One of the most famous women who ever lived, she was the last of the Ptolemaic rulers of Egypt. As "Queen of the Nile" she had love affairs with Julius Caesar and Mark Antony.

Although historians disagree concerning the accuracy of the writings of Octavian, Cleopatra's adversary and writer of most of what we know about her, historians generally agree that Cleopatra's sexual desires were not sane. She had her first sexual affair at age twelve. Once she became queen, she kept scores of men in a special house where she fed them diets that she believed would increase their sexual desires. Rumor has it that she had sexual relations with one hundred men in one night! But did her hedonism and preoccupation with pleasure fulfill her? No. She committed suicide at age thirty-nine.

History tells the story of numerous men and women who displayed abnormal and uncontrollable sexual desires. But do you realize that you and I have a problem with our sexual desires, too? The Bible reveals that the sexual desire of every one of us became warped as a result of Adam's sin. We were each born with twisted sexual desires. None of us can know what holy sexual attraction is really like. None of us can know what Adam and Eve first felt when they saw one another through pure and holy eyes.

I control my desires, you may be thinking. *I'm not like people who express excessive sexual desire in crazy ways. Don't lump me into that same mold.*

Even if you have suppressed *all* of your sexual desires, they are still warped by sin. They are not the way God originally designed them to be. That's why lust is such a tremendous problem today. Let me use the example of the automobile to emphasize my point.

Although automobiles are quite common (1992 statistics estimated 156 million automobiles in the United States alone that were not exclusively used for business, and 1996 statistics noted that sixty percent of the households in the United States had two or more cars at that time), a particular type of automobile is very rare. What is it? A race car.

Although it is by definition an auto (self) mobile (moving), it's not a normal automobile. Its engine, suspension, and other parts have been altered in order to increase its performance. A stock car, for example, looks normal on the outside; but inside it has been altered. It has more horsepower than the original car and can accelerate to speeds over two hundred miles per hour. Turbocharged cars, Formula 1 racers, and Indy cars can travel even faster. Drag-racing cars can exceed speeds of three hundred miles per hour within a short distance and require parachutes in order to stop.

The few people who own race cars don't usually drive them on normal streets because of speed limit restrictions. Imagine how difficult it would be to restrict a race car to twenty miles per hour on a city street near a school or even seventy-five miles per hour on the freeway.

Sexually speaking, we can be compared to race cars. Our engines have been altered. Our sexual desires have been inherently turbocharged, and it's difficult for many of us to function within the limits that God has established for us. This is partly because of sin in our hearts and partly because of sin all around us in the world. Bombarded by sex in movies, magazines, television programs, conversations, and advertising, our sexual desires are challenged to accelerate to insane levels.

For example, imagine a man walking onto a stage in a crowded auditorium. In his hand he carries a tray. On the tray, hidden by a veil, is an ordinary orange. He walks back and forth across the stage, and ever so slowly he begins to lift the veil. The crowd shouts wildly. The background music intensifies. The audience can hardly handle the suspense. Finally, he slips off the veil and exposes the orange. Wildly, the crowd yells and jumps up and down. When the man begins to peel the orange, the crowd totally loses control.

If you saw this happening, you'd say, "That's crazy. Those people are insane! Their normal appetite for oranges has gone amuck." You would be exactly right.

Yet sadly, that is happening today in towns and cities across our world as men jam nightclubs in order to watch a woman remove her clothing and women jam nightclubs in order to watch a man remove his clothing. *Epithumia*, the lust of excessive sexual desire, is not sane.

Lust Is Sexual Desire Without Boundaries

About three thousand years ago in Israel "in the spring, at the time when kings go off to war" (2 Samuel 11:1), King David sent his supreme military commander Joab and the Israelite army to fight the Ammonites. David, however, remained in Jerusalem in his palace.

Perhaps you know what happened next. One evening, David got up from his couch and walked around the palace roof. Suddenly, he noticed a very beautiful woman bathing on another roof. Instead of turning his eyes and mind in a different direction, David asked a servant to find out who she was.

"Isn't this Bathsheba, the daughter of Eliam and the wife of Uriah the Hittite?" the servant informed David (1 Samuel 11:3).

David could have shut down his sexual temptation again, but

he didn't. He sent messengers to bring Bathsheba to the palace. Consumed by desire, he then had sexual relations with her; and she became pregnant. David's lust, you see, had no boundaries. As Uriah's wife, Bathsheba was out of bounds sexually for any man but her husband.

Understandably, King David panicked. He knew that he was in trouble and that Uriah would find out. So the king devised a plan. He summoned Uriah from the battlefield and offered him a vacation. "Go on home," the king said, in effect, "and have some fun. You deserve it." *Any red-blooded man,* he reasoned, *would go home and have sex with his wife. Uriah will do that and think that the baby is his.*

Uriah, however, didn't go home. A zealous soldier, he refused even to see Bathsheba, for he was reminded that his fellow soldiers were at war and living in tents in the open fields.

Thus David devised another plan. He invited Uriah to eat and to drink with him in hopes that when the soldier became drunk he'd return home. But once again Uriah remained loyal to his fellow soldiers. Instead of returning home, he slept on a mat among David's servants.

Now David devised a new, more hideous plan. "Put Uriah in the front line where the fighting is fiercest," he wrote in a letter that Uriah carried to Joab. "Then withdraw from him so he will be struck down and die" (2 Samuel 11:14-15). Joab obeyed, and Uriah was killed.

Thinking that all was okay, David married Bathsheba. David's sin of lust multiplied into adultery, deceit, and murder; and God became enraged at His chosen king.

God has established clear boundaries for sexual behavior. To Him, sexuality is not dirty. It's the highest expression of physical union between a man and a woman. It's a beautiful gift that He has given to men and women; and it's meant to be opened within the context of the spiritual and emotional union of marriage.

When this gift is opened at another time in another way, it is tainted. It is cheapened. It is sinful. For the most part even the secular world in which we live acknowledges that adultery is out of bounds.

But, otherwise, most secular people recognize few "absolute" sexual boundaries. If a single man or woman is sexually attracted to another person, the world encourages him or her to "be natural," to "have fun," to "do it." God, however, says that sex before marriage (*porneia*) is fornication. It is immoral. It is out of bounds.

Many secular people say that it's okay to be a lesbian or a homosexual because sex between two people of the same gender is natural and part of the variety of human sexuality. Some respected medical doctors say that homosexuals are genetically predisposed to be homosexuals. Some respected psychologists say that homosexuality is environmentally predisposed. From a biblical perspective, however, these views don't matter. God says that sex between people of the same gender is sinful and out of bounds (Romans 1:26-27).

God is compassionate. He loves us all. He is merciful and full of grace. He understands our sexual struggles, but He challenges us to be holy and warns us against committing sexual sin. He has established boundaries for us. What He calls sin is sin.

Many men and women today choose to go outside the sexual boundaries that God has established thinking they can protect themselves from the consequences, such as AIDS, venereal disease, or an unwanted pregnancy. These people are more concerned with the consequences than they are with God's absolute truth. God, however, warns that no one will escape the consequences of not obeying His boundaries.

Not long ago I was jogging along the Highline Canal, a scenic area near my Colorado home. Although a local ordinance requires that dog owners leash their dogs in that area, a woman walking toward me didn't have her two big dogs on their leashes. One of the dogs zeroed in on me and nipped at my heels. That frightened me. I wasn't sure if I should stop jogging or keep going. Soon the dog hit the back of my legs with its paws and nearly tackled me.

Why did the woman ignore the leash law? Perhaps she figured that the odds were greater that she would not be caught. What were the odds that she'd face negative consequences? What were the odds that a park ranger would come along while she was out walking her dogs? Slim to none, right? So she didn't care.

Many people are like that. *If nobody sees what I do,* they think, *it doesn't matter if I disobey the law.* But it does matter! You see, even if that woman woke up the next morning and felt that she had done nothing wrong, she still disobeyed the law. God saw what she did.

One day God will judge our thoughts and actions. We will face consequences, whether or not we believe that. We are not free to do whatever we want to do if the consequences seem trivial or nonexistent to us. God won't judge us by our sexual predispositions but by what we choose to do with them. If we play with sinful desires in our minds and/or give in to them in our actions, we commit sin because we have moved outside God's boundaries for us.

A Personal Challenge

Lust is a difficult subject to discuss, perhaps because it's so prominent today. Virtually all of us struggle with it, for we're all fallen people. Lust is really subtle because we can commit it in our hearts even when we haven't acted inappropriately in a visible way. Jesus said in the Sermon on the Mount,

> You have heard that it was said, 'Do not commit adultery.' But I tell you that anyone who looks at a woman lustfully has already committed adultery with her in his heart.
>
> Matthew 5:22

In the *Music Box*, a movie released in 1989, Jessica Lange played the character of an attorney whose father had been accused of being a Nazi war criminal. She didn't believe it. Because she knew her father well, loved him deeply, and believed him when he denied the accusation, she agreed to defend him. As time passed, however, she began to suspect that maybe her father wasn't the man she believed him to be. She wondered if there were parts of his life that had been hidden from her and that perhaps he had committed horrible war crimes. The evidence mounted, and she discovered the facts in a music box.

Not long ago I watched a television interview of the producer of the *Music Box*. The producer of the movie explained that he wanted to show the world that no one can really know everything about another person, for he believed that every person held personal secrets in his/her mind and heart.

Do we really know everything about our spouses, our children, our ministers, our best friends, or our neighbors? Clearly not. But God does. He sees and hears everything. He knows everything about each of us, even what's in our hearts and minds.

> For there is nothing hidden that will not be disclosed,
> and nothing concealed that will not be known or
> brought out into the open.
> Luke 8:17

> Nothing in all creation is hidden from God's sight.
> Everything is uncovered and laid bare before the eyes
> of him to whom we must give account.
> Hebrews 4:13

If you really believe in Jesus Christ as your Lord and Savior, do you honestly want to please Him? Do you desire His holiness? Do you want to live a life of purity? Do you want to stand before Him one day and see Him smile? Do you want to hear Him say, "Well done, my good and faithful servant"? If so, you may have to make some changes.

Spiritual darkness in this world is growing, and the light of Christ seems strange to people who do not yet know Him. The world may not understand this; but if you want to become sane, you need to shut out the lustful influences of the world that accelerate sinful sexual desires within you. If you are reading adult sex publications, such as *Playboy*, *Playgirl*, or *Penthouse*, cancel your subscriptions or choose not to buy these magazines over the counter. If you are surfing the internet for pornographic sites, stop. You need to carefully scrutinize the movies you see. You need to be careful about the television programs you watch, the books you read, and the people with whom you associate.

God wants us to honestly examine our hearts. Is lust a problem? If it is, He wants us to confess that sin and repent. He wants us to say, "Lord, I want to change. I want to obey You. I want to follow You." God wants us to echo the prayer that David prayed in Psalm 139:23-24.

> Search me, O God, and know my heart; test me and know my anxious thoughts. See if there is any offensive way in me, and lead me in the way everlasting.

God wants to forgive us. He wants to cleanse our hearts and to give us a new start. He wants to release His power and holiness in us, but we must long to become like Him.

The old nature within us is rooted in the sinful world; the new nature within us has been given to us through Christ and is inspired by the Holy Spirit. We can choose to feed the old nature or the new nature. If we feed the old nature, we will struggle with the sin of lust. If we feed the new nature, God will give us victory over lust.

We need to choose to spend time in the Word every day. We need to choose to bathe our lives in prayer every day. We need to make choices that honor God. We need to long for Christlikeness and the transforming power of the Holy Spirit in our lives. In return, God will work in our lives in ways we never thought possible.

Let us remember the words with which this chapter began and rid our lives of lust. May we accept the Lord's calling and faithfully pursue His boundaries for our lives. Only in His strength can we find the strength to stand firm against the lust of this age.

Envy

CHAPTER FOUR

Wolfgang Amadeus Mozart, a rare genius musically, exhibited his gifts almost from the moment of his birth in 1756. The exciting and complex music he composed manifested his mastery over virtually all forms of composition. Although God had granted him unbelievable giftedness, Mozart was not devout. In fact, he was often crude, sometimes vulgar, and responded in immature ways.

Antonio Salieri was a contemporary of Mozart. Salieri lived in Vienna, Austria, and at age twenty-four was the court composer and conductor of the Italian Opera in the patronage of Joseph II. Acknowledging the majesty of God, Salieri longed to glorify God through his music. He wanted to lift the hearts of men and women toward heaven. He asked only that God allow him to compose music worthy of His great glory. Yet for whatever reason God didn't grant Salieri a magnitude of greatness. Yes, his music entertained; but he never composed an "immortal" masterpiece that stood the test of time and immortalized him.

Did Salieri remain content to serve God to the best of his abilities anyway? Did he single-mindedly focus on God and on how his music could guide people to know the Creator? Unfortunately, history reveals that just the opposite occurred. You see, the seed of envy grew within Salieri. As it took hold, he envied Mozart more and more. That envy became obsessive, and he plotted Mozart's demise.

At first the changes within Salieri were subtle; but as envy established a firm foundation in his life, he changed markedly. Instead of blessing God, he cursed Him for not granting him the magnitude of giftedness that Mozart had received. Instead of glorifying God with the talents he did possess, he placed emphasis on the genius he didn't have and on the genius that Mozart had. In the end Salieri reached the brink of insanity. His mind was eaten by envy. His faith in God crumbled. His ministry was destroyed.

Envy Involves Comparison

The Greek word *phthonos*, translated "envy" in the Bible, is always a comparative word. Envy is more than basic desire or covetousness. Envy is a unique kind of desire or covetousness that is rooted in comparison. You and I can't possibly envy unless we compare ourselves to other people. Thus the word *phthonos* in the Bible is always associated with pain because comparing ourselves to other people results in pain. No matter who we are, what we possess, whom we know, or what we look like, there will always be another person who is seemingly more blessed, more gifted, more intelligent, more wealthy, or more handsome or beautiful than we are. Therefore, when we begin to envy and compare ourselves to other people, we lose our joy and our thankfulness to God.

When asked to define envy, Sir John Gielgud, the British actor, stated, "I can define envy in this way: When Sir Laurence Olivier performed Hamlet in 1948 and the critics raved, I wept."

In 1503, the leaders of the Italian city of Florence asked Leonardo da Vinci to paint a battle scene on a wall of the great council hall in Florence. These leaders of Florence also asked a young, relatively unknown artist to paint on a wall of the council hall. He also agreed to do it. His name? Michelangelo.

When both artists completed their paintings, most viewers acknowledged that Michelangelo's painting was more spectacular than da Vinci's. As a result da Vinci was never the same. Although he lived eighteen more years and painted other great works, his influence and stature as an artist decreased while Michelangelo's increased. Why? Envy consumed da Vinci. His joy disappeared. Gloom, depression, and despair filled his remaining years.

In 1960, John F. Kennedy was elected President of the United States by a narrow margin over Richard M. Nixon. More than sixty-eight million votes had been cast, and Kennedy won by only 119,000 votes.

Immediately after Kennedy gave his inaugural address, Nixon said to Ted Sorenson, Kennedy's aide, "You know, there were some things Kennedy said in his speech that I would like to have said."

Sorenson replied, "You mean like the part where he said, 'Ask not what your country can do for you'?"

"No," Nixon answered. "I mean like the part where he said, 'I do solemnly swear . . . .'"

Obviously, Nixon coveted the presidency; but he envied more than that. He and Kennedy had been publicly compared during the first televised presidential debate as well as in voting booths throughout the United States. It was obvious to most people that Kennedy was younger, better looking, and more charming than Nixon. Nixon was well aware of those comparisons. People who knew Nixon best have shared that he greatly envied Kennedy. He envied Kennedy's youth. He envied Kennedy's looks. He envied Kennedy's charisma. He even envied Kennedy's wealth.

We have all experienced envy. We envy a neighbor who has a nicer, more reliable car. We envy a co-worker who earns more money. We envy a pastor who has a larger church. We envy a man or a woman who has a more attractive spouse. We envy a relative who travels overseas.

The Constitutional Lie

In the Declaration of Independence we read, "We hold these truths to be self-evident, that all men are created equal." These words are beautiful, high, and lofty; but there's a problem with them. They simply are not true! We are not all created equal. At birth some people are given higher intelligence. Others are given greater beauty. Still others, like Mozart, are given inordinate giftedness. Some, such as John F. Kennedy, are born into great wealth.

But most people are born with common features. Many have no real opportunities, little giftedness, little intelligence, and few resources. In fact, between half and two-thirds of the world's people suffer in poverty. They struggle to earn five hundred dollars a year. They live in scrap houses with no running water. They walk long distances to find drinking water. They toil seven days a week and receive no governmental benefits. Even if they possess great intelligence, they have few opportunities to achieve more than an elementary education. They have no retirement income to count on. They do not own a car or receive regular health care. Truly, people are not created equal.

In God's eyes, however, we are all equal. He loves each of us equally with a love we cannot fully comprehend. But He knows that we are not equally endowed. Just as He recognized Abraham's strengths and weaknesses, He knew the strengths and weaknesses of Cain, Abel, Samson, Saul, David, Peter, and the woman at the well. God gifted the craftsmen who worked on the temple, and he gifted Samuel to be His prophet to the Israelites.

In whatever way God has gifted us, He expects us to be a good steward of His gift—whether that gift is little or much. He desires that we take whatever He has entrusted to us and, with thanksgiving, cultivate it and make the most of it. Not only does He command us not to compare ourselves with others (Psalm 49:16-19, James 3:16, Job 5:2, Proverbs 14:30), but also He commands us to rejoice in whatever He has given to others (Romans 12:15, 1 Corinthians 12:26).

Envy Is a Hostile Word

According to the Bible, envy is also a hostile word because true envy always results in hostility. Let's suppose, for example, that while

Chapter Four: Envy

I'm visiting the home of a friend, I notice some furnishings I wish I had in my home —a lamp, a painting, an ornate door, a hand-carved desk.

Is it okay to wish that I possessed one or more of these items? Sure, and if I really wanted them badly enough and had enough money, maybe I could buy similar ones. But if I begrudge the fact that my friend possesses these items and wish that he didn't have them, that's a sin. When I envy, I not only want what another person has but also I don't want that person to have it.

Sadly, envy has invaded the kingdom of Christ. Denominations envy one another. Churches envy one another. Ministers envy one another. How can this be? As Christians we are to be united under Christ in one Gospel, serving His eternal kingdom until the closing of the age when we see our Lord face to face. United under our common Lord and having one Spirit, we are called to rejoice with one another and to pray for one another. Instead, envy surfaces and hostility erupts.

Perhaps you've heard the story of the family who lost a loved one. They lived in a small country town, and the minister of their thriving denomination was away on vacation. Needing someone to handle the funeral service and the burial, family members asked the minister of a smaller, less-popular denomination to officiate the service.

Taking a moment to think it over, the minister replied, "I don't know. I will need to ask a higher-ranking person in my denomination."

He e-mailed the denominational headquarters. "Is it okay for me to bury a person from another denomination?"

His denominational leader fired back a reply. "Bury all of them you can."

On the surface this simple tale is humorous, but the underlying envy is anything but humorous. Envy creates discord in small towns and in big cities across our country and throughout the world.

During the latter portion of the twelfth century, King Richard of England and King Philip II of France became good friends. Two of the most powerful men on earth, they gathered their respective armies and marched off together to fight in the Crusades to seize the Holy Land for

Christ. They won battles together and suffered setbacks together. They became friends bonded in a common cause until one fact became apparent. King Richard of England was the greater warrior. People who recognized that his military skills and courage were superior to those of King Philip II called him "Richard Coeur de Lion," Richard the Lion-Hearted.

Realizing this, King Philip II became envious. He felt pain, which began to ooze bitterness and resentment. Soon he criticized King Richard's actions, ideas, and strategies. This, in turn, led to King Philip's open rebellion against King Richard. Resolving to bury his former friend, King Philip took his armies back to France. He declared war on England and seized all the properties that King Richard owned in France, while King Richard was imprisoned by Leopold V, Duke of Austria. The five-year battle that ensued claimed many lives and ultimately resulted in King Richard's death on the battlefield in 1199.

Genesis 4:2-7 quickly takes us back to another tragedy that resulted when envy produced hostility.

> Now Abel kept flocks, and Cain worked the soil. In the course of time Cain brought some of the fruits of the soil as an offering to the Lord. But Abel brought fat portions from some of the firstborn of his flock. The Lord looked with favor on Abel and his offering, but on Cain and his offering he did not look with favor. So Cain was very angry, and his face was downcast.

> Then the Lord said to Cain, "Why are you angry? Why is your face downcast? If you do what is right, will you not be accepted? But if you do not do what is right, sin is crouching at your door; it desires to have you, but you must master it."

After enviously comparing himself to Abel, Cain experienced pain. He envied his brother's honor, and he envied his brother's recognition from God. As he begrudged Abel, Cain grew hostile and bitter. Ultimately, "while they were in the field, Cain attacked his brother Abel and killed him" (Genesis 4:8).

Perhaps you are thinking: *Well, maybe I do envy a little bit. I guess I compare myself to others more than I should. There are probably a few people I begrudge a little bit, but I'd never do something like what Philip of France did to his former friend. I'd certainly never do what Cain did to Abel.*

King Philip II and Cain exhibited their envy in physical ways. The Bible reveals, however, that envy can exhibit itself in far more subtle ways. Haven't you experienced times when you really wanted to bury someone — not physically but verbally? The Bible reveals that when we criticize people, gossip about people, or slander people we are expressing sinful hostility that is rooted in envy. Search your heart. Is this true?

In James 3:2-12, God deals with the abuse of the tongue — the power of misused words:

> If anyone is never at fault in what he says, he is a perfect man, able to keep his whole body in check.
>
> When we put bits into the mouths of horses to make them obey us, we can turn the whole animal. Or take ships as an example. Although they are so large and are driven by strong winds, they are steered by a very small rudder wherever the pilot wants to go.
>
> Likewise the tongue is a small part of the body, but it makes great boasts. Consider what a great forest is set on fire by a small spark. The tongue also is a fire, a world of evil among the parts of the body. It

corrupts the whole person, sets the whole course of his life on fire, and is itself set on fire by hell.

All kinds of animals, birds, reptiles and creatures of the sea are being tamed and have been tamed by man, but no man can tame the tongue. It is a restless evil, full of deadly poison.

With the tongue we praise our Lord and Father, and with it we curse men, who have been made in God's likeness. Out of the same mouth come praise and cursing. My brothers, this should not be. Can both fresh water and salt water flow from the same spring? My brothers, can a fig tree bear olives, or a grapevine bear figs? Neither can a salt spring produce fresh water.

Notice now the next few verses, James 3:13-16:

Who is wise and understanding among you? Let him show it by his good life, by deeds done in the humility that comes from wisdom. But if you harbor bitter envy and selfish ambition in your hearts, do not boast about it or deny the truth. Such "wisdom" does not come down from heaven but is earthly, unspiritual, of the devil. For where you have envy and selfish ambition, there you find disorder and every evil practice.

Clearly, if we understand and believe these words, we know that the abuse of the tongue is rooted in envy — as are so many other hostile attitudes and actions. We must search our hearts and minds, using God's power, and uproot any seeds of envy that we have allowed to be nourished in our lives. Otherwise, what happened to Salieri, da Vinci, Nixon, King Phillip II, and Cain will happen to us. God will grieve, not only because of the sins that result but also because of what the sins displace in our lives — the joy, the peace, and the other fruit of the Spirit.

Gluttony
CHAPTER FIVE

Although the scientific name of this fur-bearing animal is *gulo gulo*, Europeans and Asians call it the glutton. The largest member of the weasel family, the glutton lives in the northern forests and tundra of Europe, Asia, and North America. About three-and-a-half feet long and weighing up to fifty-five pounds, a full-grown glutton has a voracious appetite and can kill animals as large as caribou and deer. How does such a relatively small animal bring down these much larger animals? The glutton pounces on the back of its prey and uses its powerful claws to shred the flesh until the animal falls. Because the word *glutton* sounds quite offensive here in the United States, this animal is called by another name, the wolverine.

What Is Gluttony?

The biblical word translated "gluttony" is *phagos*, which simply means "to eat too much, to overeat." Gluttony is the act of over-indulgence and normally refers to the practice of habitually eating too much food during extended periods of time. It's not simply a momentary binge at Thanksgiving or Christmas.

The odds are that you haven't heard of Robert Earl Hughes, born in Monticello, Illinois, in 1926. At age six he weighed 203 pounds—not your average first grader! At age ten he weighed 378 pounds. At age thirteen he weighed 576 pounds. At age eighteen he weighed 696 pounds. At age twenty-five he weighed 896 pounds. At age twenty-seven he weighed 945 pounds. When he died at age thirty-two, he weighed 1,041 pounds. He was buried in a piano case and lowered into the ground with a crane.

How did Robert become so obese? Did he live a sedentary lifestyle? Was he born with a genetic tendency toward obesity? Did he suffer from the disease that attacks the endocrine gland or the satiety centers of the brain, which affects the satiation of appetite? Were there physiological and emotional factors? Although we do not know with certainty all the reasons that contributed to Robert's obesity, one factor is clear: He overindulged in eating. For a snack, he would eat three or four chickens. When he had a salad, he sometimes ate it out of a wheelbarrow.

Often, however, gluttonous people are not as easy to distinguish as Robert must have been. In fact, some gluttonous people overindulge regularly but don't look overweight, and their reasons for overeating may vary widely. People may overeat because they are bored, and eating is something to do. They may overeat because they are lonely, and eating makes them feel better. They may overeat because their self-esteem is low, and they use food to say, "I love you," to themselves. They may overeat because they feel anxious, and eating provides a sense of comfort. They may overeat simply because food tastes good or because food serves as their primary reward system. They may even overeat because they were taught to do so by their parents!

When my brothers and I were young, my dad taught us to overeat. I loved and respected my dad very much, and he was a great man. But during the 1950's and 1960's, he believed what many other people believed — the more you ate, the healthier you were.

My dad didn't simply want us to finish the food on our plates when we ate at an all-you-can-eat restaurant. He wanted us to get another plate and fill it up. It was like a war, and there were winners and losers. The winner wasn't simply the person who ate the most —

although my dad loved to laughingly say that I "had a hollow leg" if I went back for a third plate of food. Rather the entire family won if we made the restaurant lose. If we ate twenty dollars worth of food and paid only five dollars, he deemed the meal a success. As I reflect back on those years, I think my brothers and I overate in order to please my dad.

When I married Barbara, I weighed 210 pounds — well within the normal weight range for my age, height, and body frame. But one year later I weighed 240 pounds, and I had gained that weight very easily! I was studying hard in my doctoral program. To compensate, I rewarded myself with food every night. Many nights at 11 p.m., while watching previously played U.C.L.A. basketball games or late-night television programs, I would consume four golden-brown cherry or raspberry turnovers right out of the oven and down two glasses of whole milk.

Barbara and I just thought I was "big" until we traveled to Europe at the end of that year. After we returned and I looked at the slides we'd taken of our trip, I thought, *Wow, is that me?* In a slide of me walking down a little, narrow street in France, it looked as if my shoulders were hitting the walls on both sides of the street! Only then did I realize that I had committed the sin of gluttony. I had over-indulged, and I knew I needed to take my weight seriously and lose those excessive pounds.

Why Is Gluttony Sinful?

Michel Lotito has been called the world's greatest omnivore. (That means he eats all kinds of food.) But his definition of food is quite different from the definition of most people. Born in Grenoble, France, in 1950, Michel began eating metal and glass at age nine. According to gastroenterologists, who have examined him through x-rays and other tests, he can actually consume two pounds of metal a day and get away with it! Since 1966, he has eaten ten bicycles, seven television sets, and six chandeliers. In four-and-a-half days he ate a supermarket shopping cart. He has also eaten a Cessna light aircraft! One could say that it might be easier for him to eat an airplane than to go through an airport metal detector before boarding an airplane.

As my son Drew and I read about Michel in the *Guinness Book of World Records*, Drew asked this appropriate question: "Why would anybody want to do this?" Metal and glass don't even taste good, after all, and are extremely dangerous to the human body.

Yes, this is an extreme case, and such actions could prove to be fatal. Yet many people harm their bodies in a more culturally acceptable way by chronically eating too much. Medical and scientific evidence reveal that people who regularly overindulge when they eat are more susceptible to illness and disease. High blood pressure, strokes, heart attacks, and some forms of cancer have all been linked to overindulgence in food.

"Why can't I eat as much as I want to eat?" someone might ask. "I mean, I'm not hurting anyone. Why is gluttony a sin, anyway?"

The moment we invited Jesus Christ to sit on the throne of our lives and to be our Savior from sin, He sent His Holy Spirit to reside within us; and we became spiritually reborn. Our physical bodies have become temples of God.

> Don't you know that you yourselves are God's temple and that God's Spirit lives in you? If anyone destroys God's temple, God will destroy him; for God's temple is sacred, and you are that temple.
>
> 1 Corinthians 3:16-17

> Do you not know that your body is a temple of the Holy Spirit, who is in you, whom you have received from God? You are not your own; you were bought at a price. Therefore honor God with your body.
>
> 1 Corinthians 6:19-20

Chapter Five: Gluttony

Whenever we do anything that willfully harms our human bodies without just cause, we commit sin. God the Creator created our bodies. When we overindulge and damage our bodies, we are truly damaging the temple of God. God challenges us to offer our bodies as living sacrifices that are holy and pleasing to Him (Romans 12:1).

Our physical health is serious business to the Lord; and, therefore, God cares deeply about how we take care of our physical bodies. When we overindulge, we hurt the bodies He created. We desecrate His temple. We mock the One who died on the cross for us so that we might have eternal life. Because gluttony (or any other form of overindulgence) damages the body over a period of time, it is sinful.

How Do We Overcome Our Overindulgences?

The Bible offers some practical guidelines on how we can overcome our overindulgences.

Confess and Repent of Our Sin

First of all, the Bible reveals that in order to overcome gluttony we must acknowledge that it is a sin. If we don't believe it's a sin, we'll not take it seriously; and we'll never gain victory over it.

Then, we must confess our sin to God. "If we confess our sins," God promises that He will be "faithful and just and will forgive us our sins and purify us from all unrighteousness" (1 John 1:9).

After God forgives us, we must choose to repent — to turn away from the sinful habit of overindulgence and to pursue a different, godly direction. As we offer our bodies as living sacrifices to Him, He can begin to renew and transform the way we think (Romans 12:1-2).

Pray

Next, God wants us to share with Him our deepest needs, longings, and problems. According to the Bible, prayer makes a difference. God said to Jeremiah, "Call to me, and I will answer you and tell you great and unsearchable things you do not know" (Jeremiah 33:3).

In Luke 18:1-8, Jesus told His disciples to continue to pray until God answered. Hebrews 4:16 tells us to "approach the throne of grace with confidence, so that we may receive mercy and find grace to help us in our time of need."

In 1 John 3:22, God promises to give us what we pray for when we obey His commands and do what pleases Him. Proverbs 15:8 reveals that the prayers of upright people please God. God is, as Paul wrote, "able to do immeasurably more than all we ask or imagine, according to his power that is at work within us" (Ephesians 3:20).

Do you really want to stop overindulging? If so, you need to harness the power of prayer. You need to "be joyful in hope, patient in affliction, *faithful in prayer*" (Romans 12:12, italics added).

All habitual and chronic sin, including overindulgence, can lead to a form of bondage and tends to be related to spiritual problems. Sometimes even Satan himself has trapped us in a kind of spiritual bondage. Therefore, we need to pray and ask others to pray for us (because there is great power in intercessory prayer) that God will set us free from our bondage so that we can experience the liberty He desires to give us.

Exercise Self-Control

Since the beginning of time, the world as a whole has suffered from *akrates*, the biblical word that means "having no self-control." In the Bible gluttony is sometimes associated with drunkenness (Matthew 11:19, Proverbs 23:20-21). The Bible also associates gluttony with lying and evil (Titus 1:12). Why is gluttony mentioned with these other sins? We gain understanding when we examine the Greek and the Roman world to-which the Gospel message first went. It was a world in which people exercised little or no self-control. Men attended pagan temple parties where food and wine were served without limit. Fertility goddesses and temple prostitutes were abundant, and partygoers gratified their sexual appetites through immorality and idol worship. Over and over again, however, the Bible exhorts and admonishes

Christians to exercise self-control:

Addressing the importance of controlling one's temper, Solomon wrote, "Better a patient man than a warrior, a man who controls his temper than one who takes a city (Proverbs 16:32).

When the Gospel message spread, people who embraced Christ as their Lord and Savior received a mandate to exercise self-control: "Make every effort to add to your faith, goodness; and to goodness, knowledge; and to knowledge, *self-control*" (2 Peter 1:5-6, italics added).

Recognizing the power of sin and how easily sinful habits can become rooted in a Christian's life, Paul wrote, "Therefore do not let sin reign in your mortal body so that you obey its evil desires. . . . Let us behave decently, as in the daytime, not in orgies and drunkenness, not in sexual immorality and debauchery, not in dissension and jealousy" (Romans 6:12; 13:13).

Writing to Titus, Paul listed self-control as an essential qualification of eldership: "Since an overseer is entrusted with God's word, . . . he must be hospitable, one who loves what is good, who is *self-controlled*, upright, holy and disciplined" (Titus 1:7-8, italics added).

Although not everyone will admit it, virtually every person has some capacity to exercise self-control. As Christians we have an even greater capacity because the Holy Spirit resides in us and provides us with real power. In Galatians 5:22-23 we read, "The fruit of the Spirit is love, joy, peace, patience, kindness, goodness, faithfulness, gentleness and *self-control*" (italics added).

If you and I really set our wills to do His will, we can draw on the spiritual strength God provides. Yes, exercising self-control can be painful or at least difficult, but God provides the power we need to achieve victory.

Seek out the Support of Other Christians

Certainly, a number of Christians today cannot stop overindulging. They wrestle, for example, with eating disorders, such as anorexia, bulimia, or simply overeating; yet they are trying to honor

God with their bodies. They have confessed their sin of overindulgence and have repented. They have prayed and asked God to strengthen their resolve and to fill them with His power. They have tried to exercise self-control, yet they are still losing the battle. They are not receiving victory. They are still overindulging and need help.

Fortunately, God has provided each of us with other believers who love us and who will help us. Knowing our tendency to be self-sufficient, He has, in fact, told us that we need the support of other Christians, our brothers and sisters in Christ.

In the book of Hebrews, we are challenged to "encourage one another daily" (Hebrews 3:13) and to "not give up meeting together, as some are in the habit of doing, but [to] encourage one another—and all the more as [we] see the Day approaching" (Hebrews 10:25).

Recognizing the importance of fellowship and accountability, Paul charged Timothy in 2 Timothy 4:2 to "preach the Word; [to] be prepared in season and out of season; [to] correct, rebuke and encourage—with great patience and careful instruction."

Writing to the believers in Ephesus, Paul challenged them to "speak to one another with psalms, hymns and spiritual songs" (Ephesians 5:19).

Even the secular world acknowledges the importance of people meeting together to support one another and to encourage personal accountability. That's why so many people participate in self-help organizations. As Christians we also need support and accountability. God wants us to draw together with other brothers and sisters in Christ. He wants us to seek out qualified people when we need godly counsel. Above all, He wants us to choose to live lives that honor and please Him. He wants us to choose to honor Him with our bodies, souls, and spirits.

A Final Challenge

On March 20, 1947, a female blue whale was killed. Its heart weighed 1,540 pounds. Its tongue weighed 19,500 pounds. In total the whale weighed 418,000 pounds! How did this blue whale become so

Chapter Five: Gluttony

large? An average blue whale needs three million calories a day, but this particular whale overindulged and consumed an estimated four to five million calories a day!

Of course, there is a huge difference between an overindulgent whale that cannot be held morally accountable and human beings who are morally accountable to God. We have true volition. Created in God's image, we can make choices. For example, we can choose to honor God, or we can seek to live according to our sinful desires. We can choose to seek help from other Christians in the body of Christ when we're having trouble with gluttony, or we can try to succeed on our own.

Do you remember what Joshua said to all the tribes of Israel at Shechem? After reminding them of God's covenant and what He had done for them, Joshua challenged them with these words:

> Now fear the Lord and serve him with all faithfulness. Throw away the gods your forefathers worshiped beyond the River and in Egypt, and serve the Lord. But if serving the Lord seems undesirable to you, then choose for yourselves this day whom you will serve, . . . But as for me and my household, we will serve the Lord.
>
> Joshua 24:14-15

Everyday we have the same choice Joshua offered the Israelites. Will we choose to serve God? Will we make choices that honor Him. Will we take care of the temple, our bodies, in which the Holy Spirit lives? Will we choose to repent of our sin, to pray, to exercise self-control, and to be active in the body of Christ? We must choose today whom we will serve!

Sloth

Have you ever watched honey bees in a field or at a nature center as they zip to and fro gathering pollen? If so, you know where the expression "busy as a bee" comes from! In order to make one pound of honey, more than 550 worker honey bees must gather nectar from more than 2,500,000 flowers. Depending on the location of the flowers to their hive, honey bees may easily travel a collective distance of twice the circumference of the earth.

Unfortunately, some people are not as motivated as honey bees are. They are downright lazy—slothful. More than 1,900 years ago, during the days of the apostle Paul, many people in the city of Thessalonica had quit their jobs and were living in idleness. The Greek translation of the words describing their idleness, *Ergazomai peri ergazomai*, means "working around working."

We don't know why these people chose not to earn their living. Perhaps they believed that the Lord's coming was imminent. Whatever the reason, however, the Thessalonians' slothfulness caused Paul to strongly rebuke them and to command them to return to work. He also commanded those who were working not to support those who were slothful. We read in 2 Thessalonians 3:6-12 the following exhortation:

In the name of the Lord Jesus Christ, we command you, brothers, to keep away from every brother who is idle and does not live according to the teaching you received from us.

For you yourselves know how you ought to follow our example. We were not idle when we were with you, nor did we eat anyone's food without paying for it. On the contrary, we worked night and day, laboring and toiling so that we would not be a burden to any of you. We did this, not because we do not have the right to such help, but in order to make ourselves a model for you to follow. For even when we were with you, we gave you this rule: "If a man will not work, he shall not eat."

We hear that some among you are idle. They are not busy; they are busybodies. Such people we command and urge in the Lord Jesus Christ to settle down and earn the bread they eat.

Among most subcultures in the United States and other advanced countries, few people exhibit this type of sloth. Most people are willing to work and to earn a living. Even most unemployed people are in-between jobs and are pursuing future employment because they want to work. But sloth exhibits itself in ways other than not working that can be more dangerous to all of us.

Being Too Lazy to Love

One day an expert in the religious law tried to test the Lord Jesus Christ (Luke 10:25-28). "Teacher, what must I do to inherit eternal life?" he asked.

Jesus responded with a question, "What is written in the Law?

How do you read it?"

The expert replied, "'Love the Lord your God with all your heart and with all your soul and with all your strength and with all your mind'; and, 'Love your neighbor as yourself.'"

Jesus stated, "You have answered correctly. Do this and you will live."

But when the expert asked Jesus to define the word *neighbor*, Jesus illustrated the word with the familiar story we call the Parable of the Good Samaritan (Luke 10:30-37).

In this parable thieves attacked a man traveling from Jerusalem to Jericho. They "stripped him of his clothes, beat him and went away, leaving him half dead" (vs. 30). A priest came by, saw the wounded man, and passed on the other side of the road. A Levite, a descendant of the priestly lineage of Levi, also walked by on the other side of the road. Finally, a Samaritan came by. Instead of continuing on his way, this good man took pity on the injured traveler.

The Samaritan did what love required. He walked over to the wounded man. He poured medicinal oil on the wounds and bandaged them. He lifted the man onto a donkey and took him to a distant inn. There the Samaritan stayed up all night giving medical care to the injured man. In the morning he paid the innkeeper two silver coins so that the innkeeper could continue to provide medical care to the injured man. Before leaving, he committed himself to return and to pay for any additional expenses incurred by the innkeeper. "Look after him," the Samaritan stated, "and when I return, I will reimburse you for any extra expense you may have" (vs. 35).

People have asked, "Why didn't the priest or the Levite respond like that? Why did they keep walking?"

Suggested answers vary. Maybe they didn't do what love required because they thought the wounded man was dead and, in accordance with Judaic law, didn't want to become defiled and ceremonially unclean by touching a dead body. Maybe they were late for a temple ceremony or some other ecclesiastical function. Maybe, as some people have suggested tongue in cheek, they saw that the man had already been robbed and had nothing else to give.

But I think the following answer may be the most accurate one: The priest and the Levite passed by because of sloth. They were simply too lazy to love! They knew the work that love required, and they simply didn't want to do it. Love always requires work, and some people are simply too lazy to love.

This truth is sadly illustrated in many marriage relationships today. Marriage, according to the Bible, is founded on a special kind of love. This love requires a commitment. This love is a decision to meet one another's needs until death. Yet today many people speak of love as something you "fall into" and "fall out of."

Anthony Campolo, an author and professor, tells a story about a man who was both a high school and college athlete. Dave (not his real name) loved sports; and if he was not playing, then he was at an arena or in front of the television soaking in the action.

One day he met a beautiful woman. They fell in love and married. Even though she didn't really enjoy sports, she worked at becoming a sports fan in order to enter his sports world. She attended college and professional sporting events with him. She watched sports on television with him. She even read the sports page so she could converse with him.

As time passed, Dave's obsession with sports became his life. He spent every free weekday and weekend minute immersed in sports. He lost interest in church activities. He lost interest in family activities. He even lost interest in his wife. He stopped paying genuine attention to her; he did not seek to meet her needs; and he lost all sexual interest in her. In time she fell in love with another man.

"What can I do to get my wife back?" he asked Anthony. "Is there something I can do?"

Anthony replied, "There is one thing you can do. You can love your wife. It's going to be work, but you can love your wife. You can cut back on sports — the number of sporting events you attend and the amount of time you spend watching sports on television. Begin to involve yourself with your family at church and in your home. Participate in family activities and serve the needs of your wife. Wake up every day and ask yourself, 'What can I do to serve her? What can I do to make her happy?' That's what you can do."

Dave replied, "Well, honestly, I've thought of all that. To tell you the truth, I'm not sure it's worth the effort. I want her back but not that much."

Admittedly, this is an extreme example, but it illustrates the tragedy that occurs when people are too lazy to love. This type of slothfulness, to a lesser degree, is epidemic today. Many people are simply too lazy to do what love requires.

Being Too Lazy to Nurture

Sloth also threatens us because it contributes to the breakdown of our families. God tells fathers in Ephesians 6:4 to bring up their children "in the training and instruction of the Lord." Yet Jesus revealed that as we approach Armageddon and His second coming "the love of most [including parents] will grow cold" (Matthew 24:12) and "children will rebel against their parents" (Matthew 10:21).

As we look around us, certainly there is a lack of parental nurturing within many families today. In fact, if those of us who are parents are honest, our children may be nurtured by television and by their peers to a much greater degree than we'd like. Some of us have abdicated much of our nurturing responsibilities. In general, most children in this country are being nurtured by a secular world—secular media and peers. Let's consider some startling statistics reported by various studies in the United States:

- By the time the average child reaches age eighteen, he or she will have witnessed more than fifteen thousand murders on television or in the movies. Today there is more brutal violence and explicit sex on television than ever before.

• In 1970, ninety percent of white children under age eighteen lived with both parents. In 1995, that percentage dropped to seventy-six percent. Among black families the percentage during the same time period dropped from fifty-nine percent to thirty-three percent. Overall, fewer than sixty percent of all children live with their biological, married parents.

• In 1960, about 463,000 children were affected by divorce. In 1991, that number rose to 985,000.

• In 1976, about 669,000 cases of child abuse were reported. In 1991, that number escalated to an estimated 2,694,000 reported cases.

• In 1995, nearly nine thousand people between the ages of fifteen and twenty-four committed suicide. Since 1960, the teen suicide rate has more than tripled, making suicide the third leading cause of death among adolescents. Even more startling is the fact that there may be fifty to one hundred adolescent suicide attempts for every successful suicide.

• According to the University of Michigan's twenty-second annual survey of American high school seniors and sixth annual survey of eighth- and tenth-grade students, drug use among youth continued to rise in 1996. Nearly forty-five percent of America's high school seniors (class of 1996) had used marijuana, and more than eighty percent had used alcohol. Among eighth-graders more than twenty-five percent had used alcohol within the month before the survey was taken.

• According to the Federal Bureau of Investigation, the fastest growing segment of the criminal population is our nation's children. Violent crime arrest rates rose from 137 per 100,000 in

1960 to more than 430 per 100,000 in 1990. Children younger than ten, according to the Federal Bureau of Investigation, have actually been arrested and convicted of rape and murder. Violence is growing in our homes, in our schools, and in our neighborhoods.

• In 1975, sixty-three teenage girls per thousand became pregnant, and of those thirty-two had abortions. In 1990, the numbers jumped to about ninety-nine girls per thousand with an estimated forty-four abortions. According to the American Enterprise Institute, teenage sexual activity will result in nearly one million pregnancies annually, leading to approximately 406,000 abortions; 134,000 miscarriages; and 490,000 live births.

If we add further statistics, such as the number of children who run away from home every year, the number of children reported missing every year, and the number of homeless children, it'd be even more obvious that many children are not being nurtured at home by a caring family member.

Americans face a great challenge, especially in light of economic circumstances. Many parents work outside the home. Many mothers work because of economic necessity. They are single, widowed, divorced, or married to men who are unemployed or under-employed. Obviously, daycare centers are necessary, and thousands of children in the United States are in daycare centers every workday. Although daycare centers are a great help, staff members will never nurture children in the way that mothers and fathers are called to nurture them.

If we are going to nurture our children, we will have to make sacrifices. It will require a lot of work. It's not always convenient to do family activities together, which include family devotions and meals. It's not always convenient to discipline our children and to establish boundaries for their sake. It's not always convenient to monitor what our children are doing. It's so much easier to allow them to do what they want to do and to let them go where they want to go.

When I was growing up, I liked to listen to the Beatles, Elvis Presley, and the Mamas and the Papas. My parents didn't like that, though. They didn't like the way the musicians looked nor did they like the beat of the music. But those are tame issues compared to some issues related to music today.

I don't want to demean music as a whole. I also know that there will always be a gap between the musical tastes of children and the musical tastes of their parents. But some musicians today have pushed the levels of indecency, violence, and Satanism much further than musicians did previously.

Today there are so-called black metal, death metal, gloom rock, and Satanic rock groups. Musical groups in this nation perform concerts during which they simulate slashings, stabbings, and decapitations. Musicians drink blood on stage. They gnaw on animal bones. They participate in occult rituals and Satanic rites. Their lyrics can be absolutely abominable, promoting sexual promiscuity, violence, anger, and hate. Do you know what types of music your children are listening to when they shut themselves off in their rooms?

My wife Barbara and I know firsthand that child rearing is not easy and that sometimes it seems like a thankless task. But if we don't nurture our children, other people and influences will fill that void. We must not sacrifice our children on the altar of sloth. God told us to bring them up in the training and instruction of the Lord.

Many parents seek instant gratification, and child rearing doesn't offer that. Conversely, many parents serve their children, but their children are not thankful. As I look back , I often did not appreciate what my mother and father did for me while I was growing up.

During college I competed in track and field meets as far as three hundred miles from where my parents lived. Virtually every time I entered a stadium to compete, my parents would be in the stands to cheer me on. Sometimes I waved to them. Sometimes I didn't. After each meet I went off with my teammates rather then spend any time with my parents before they drove home. I just thought that my parents were doing what all parents did. I didn't realize how special it was for them to attend my meets. I didn't realize that their attendance reflected the deep love in their hearts for me.

When I was about thirty years old and had a child of my own, I began to appreciate what my parents did for me. I began to say, "thank you," and I began to tell them, "I love you."

If you are a parent, I hope that you will live long enough to hear your children call you blessed (Proverbs 31:28). I hope that you will live long enough to hear them say, "thank you." I hope that you will live long enough to hear them say, as adults, "I love you." But even if you don't live that long, God has called you to faithfully nurture your children now. Even if you never hear your children say, "thank you," God has called you to "bring them up in the nurture of the Lord" (Ephesians 6:4).

Can I promise that if you nurture your children correctly, they will turn out great? No. Life doesn't always work out like that. After all, the first people whom God created, Adam and Eve, experienced the heartache of their first born son murdering their second born son.

Despite the challenges, though, God is calling parents to faithfully nurture their children. If ever there was a generation in which parents needed to be sacrificially faithful, it's this generation. Sloth kills nurturing child rearing.

Too Lazy to Grow

Have you ever wondered where the term "sloth" comes from? It's closely linked to an animal in South America called a sloth. Hanging upside down in a tree, a sloth sleeps about eighty percent of the time. When awake, it barely moves because its metabolism converts food to energy so slowly. In fact, a sloth traveling on the ground has an average speed of seven-tenths of a mile per hour —a little more than twice the speed of a garden snail and less than twice the speed of a giant tortoise.

Sloth not only makes us too lazy to love and to nurture but also it makes us too lazy to change. It makes us too lazy to experience spiritual sanctification and transformation. It makes us too lazy to grow spiritually and to become like Christ, even though our Father in heaven desires that each of us who truly believe in Christ become Christlike. He longs for us to be conformed to the image of His Son (Romans 8:29).

What does it mean to be like Christ? It means we have His character. It means we have in our lives the fruit of the Spirit, nine attributes of Christ that God desires for us: "love, joy, peace, patience, kindness, goodness, faithfulness, gentleness, and self-control" (Galatians 5:22-23). That's the target for which God wants each of us to strive.

Every day when we wake up, we should review the fruit of the Spirit and ask ourselves, *How am I doing? Am I slothful, or am I growing? Am I becoming more like the Lord Jesus Christ? Am I growing spiritually? Am I being transformed into the image of Christ?*

We each have the opportunity right now to take action — to love, to nurture, and to grow. The choice is ours alone to make.

Anger

CHAPTER SEVEN

Since the invention of the automobile, drivers have experienced frustrations and challenges: stalled cars, flat tires, traffic jams, slippery pavement, and, of course, the consequences of arriving late at one's destination. The media has coined phrases to describe road-related situations: "traffic-monitoring skyrover helicopters," "the mousetrap," "stop and go," "increasing volume," and "fender benders" to mention a few. But today a new term is being used frequently: "road rage." This term illustrates that the nature of driving has changed. Rather than being a way to travel from one destination to another, driving—for some people—has become a way to express anger.

While driving his car during rush hour on a Philadelphia expressway, Rick (not his real name) grew increasingly frustrated. Traffic was backed up. Two lanes had narrowed into one lane in front of a construction zone, and he was in the wrong lane. After waiting fifteen minutes to merge into the lane that was moving, Rick's frustration had boiled into anger. Finally, when he had his chance to merge, another car sped around the shoulder of the road and cut in front of him.

Rick honked his horn. The guy in front of him turned around and laughed. Rick's anger intensified, and he honked again. Once again the guy in front of him turned around. This time he gestured obscenely.

Rick's anger was now out of control. He followed the car until the congestion brought all cars to a stop. Then he opened his glove compartment, removed a pistol, walked to the door of the car in front of him, and fatally shot the driver.

Why did he do it? "I just couldn't control my anger," he said later. Tired of the injustices of the freeway day after day, he just couldn't handle it when the other driver humiliated him with a taunting laugh and an obscene gesture.

Unfortunately, anger is being expressed more and more often on highways throughout our nation. Drivers weave dangerously through traffic. Horns blare; people yell; and fists or pistols, all too often, end arguments with tragic results.

We live in a world in which many people have a difficult time controlling anger. Ironically, we also live in a world that offers more and more advice on how to control it. Bookstores contain volumes of titles on anger. Men and women offer practical seminars, workbooks, and tape series on anger. Even radio and television programs focus on anger. Let's explore some of the world's practical advice concerning anger in light of Scripture.

"Suppress Your Anger"

Imagine that you are at home and have been enraged. In fact, you are yelling. Maybe you are yelling at your spouse. Maybe you are yelling at your children. Maybe you are yelling at God or at life itself. You have lost your temper.

Suddenly, the telephone rings. The call is for you. Isn't it amazing how quickly the inflection in your voice can change when you pick up the receiver? Your voice is calm, and you carry on a pleasant conversation with the person on the other end of the line. How did you manage to control your temper? You exercised self-control.

Each of us needs it. We all have it. But none of us has enough self-control to suppress anger indefinitely. If we apply the advice we receive from some people to suppress it, push it down, bury it within, and not let it out, eventually, this will backfire on us.

One winter night in Massachusetts, a man named John Stanley decided to put another log into his burning fireplace. A moment later a huge blast blew a two-inch hole in the fireplace screen and in the ceiling. Fortunately, John was not injured. Investigators later discovered that the log he had placed on the fire had been removed from the site of a World War II munitions testing range. A live twenty-millimeter shell from an anti-aircraft gun had been embedded in that log for more than forty years. It had lost none of its power.

Anger is like that shell. When you or I suppress it, it becomes embedded within us but loses none of its power. It becomes a time bomb waiting to explode. Like an explosive that becomes increasingly unstable as time passes, anger that is kept inside us can also lead to dangerous instability.

One of two reactions happens when we bottle up our anger. It can erupt explosively and uncontrollably, just as it did on that Philadelphia expressway; or it can become a slow poison that eats away at our soul causing depression, chronic anxiety, or some other disease. In fact, scientists have discovered links between long term suppressed anger and heart disease.

Interestingly, nowhere in the Bible does God tell us to suppress our anger. In fact, the Bible reveals that the opposite principle is true. God, who understands how vitally important it is for us not to suppress anger, expressed this truth: "Do not let the sun go down while you are still angry" (Ephesians 4:26). God wants us to deal with our anger. He doesn't want us to suppress it — not even for a night!

"Vent Your Anger"

This is another piece of advice promoted by many counselors and psychologists today. They want you to vent your anger in seemingly harmless ways. "If you are angry at your boss and really would like to hit him, play golf and pretend that the golf ball is your boss. If your child is angry at you and feels like hitting you, give your child a teddy bear to hit. Let your child pretend the teddy bear is you."

Vice & Virtue: The Battle Within

At first glance this advice seems valid. Anger, after all, is a strong emotion that has physiological effects. When you are angry, your respiration deepens, your pulse quickens, and your blood pressure rises. Blood in your veins is redirected from your stomach and intestines to your heart, central nervous system, and muscles. Sugar is released from the storehouse of your liver. Adrenaline is secreted. In effect, your body prepares itself for battle. So why not release your anger and allow your body to get back to normal?

Certainly, it's safer to hit a golf ball than to hit your boss. Certainly, hitting a teddy bear is better than hitting Mom. But the Bible doesn't say to vent anger. Sometimes that type of response to anger backfires.

You may remember watching John McEnroe play tennis on television. On the one hand, you may remember him for the numerous awards he won, including the Singles Crown at Wimbledon in 1981, 1983, and 1984 and three straight U.S. Open Crowns (the first man to do this since Bill Tilden). On the other hand, you may remember him for his angry outbursts on the court, such as the time he lost his temper during the Wimbledon competition in 1981 and was fined several thousand dollars.

The Bible contains many illustrations of people who vented their anger and suffered negative consequences. Cain fully vented his anger when he killed Abel, and God's judgment followed (Genesis 4:10-16). Moses vented his anger by killing an Egyptian rather than waiting for God to liberate His people from slavery. To protect himself, Moses fled Egypt (Exodus 2:11-15). King Saul vented his anger by throwing a spear at his son Jonathan because Jonathan had sided with David (1 Samuel 20:30-33.)

George Herbert Mead, an American philosopher and social psychologist, completed studies in which he discovered that venting anger is not as effective as was previously thought. Children who punched teddy bears while pretending to be hitting their mothers, for example, ended up experiencing even more anger in the long run. Their anger increased because their feelings not only influenced their actions but also their actions influenced their feelings. By participating in the action of hitting teddy bears, they actualy nurtured the anger deeper inside themselves.

If the suppression of anger and the venting of anger are not effective ways to deal with this emotion, what are the alternatives? The Bible offers us several guidelines.

Use Anger Constructively to Impact Your World for Christ

If a male athlete vents his anger by punching his coach, spitting at a referee, or taking a cheap shot at an opponent with a hockey stick, consequences must be faced. Perhaps he will be suspended from the game or have his contract terminated. Perhaps he will have to pay a steep fine. Perhaps he will lose the emotional support of his team members. But if that same athlete learns how to use his anger constructively, he can actually enhance his performance.

Martin Luther wrote these words concerning his use of anger:

> I never work better than when I am inspired by anger.
> When I am angry, I can write. I pray. I preach well.
> For then my whole temperament is quickened. My
> understanding sharpened. All mundane vexations
> and temptations depart.

Although perhaps overstating the benefits of anger, Luther understood that anger can be used for good, particularly when that anger is righteous.

Quoting Psalm 4:4, the apostle Paul wrote, "In your anger do not sin" (Ephesians 4:26). As Christians we can use our anger for good. God clearly illustrated this truth in His hatred toward sin. He became angry at His people when they complained about their hardships and weren't satisfied with the manna He had provided (Numbers 11). He became angry when they disobeyed His commands and kept items from the city of Jericho (Joshua 7:1). He became angry when they consulted false gods (2 Chronicles 25:14-15).

God, however, didn't suppress His anger and bury it for eternity. Nor did He simply vent it by arbitrarily cursing or wreaking havoc in people's lives. Rather He responded by sending His Son into our world so that Jesus could die for our sins, rise from the dead, and offer each of us His forgiveness and eternal life in heaven.

In the New Testament we read about various times in which Jesus, the Son of God, became righteously angry. One by one, He overturned the coin-laden tables of the money changers in the temple and used a whip to drive out the sheep and cattle (Matthew 21:12, John 2:14-16). He was committed to preserving the holiness of the temple. Upon seeing the hypocrisy and sinfulness of the teachers of the law and the Pharisees, Jesus angrily denounced them (Matthew 23), calling them a "brood of vipers" and telling them that they would never escape hell.

Standing outside the tomb of Lazarus, Jesus became angry at sin and death. He saw the suffering, hurt, tears, and woundedness of the people (John 11). He was, as the Greek word *embrimaomai* expresses it, "vexed in his soul." Like Jesus, we too are called to respond righteously when we experience sin, suffering, hurt, and woundedness.

When you feel righteous indignation toward the evil that's in the world, God doesn't want you to simply curse the darkness. He wants you to symbolically light a candle that will dispel spiritual darkness. He wants you to use your righteous anger to make a positive difference in people's lives.

What makes you angry? Does wholesale abortion make you angry? Does the terrible toll that drugs are having on America's chidren anger you? What about the way movies and television promote sexual permissiveness and promiscuity? How do you feel about the breakdown of the family? About poverty? If you care at all, something relating to the consequences of sin makes you angry; and God is calling you to use that anger righteously by channeling it into a ministry in which you can impact this world for good.

Chapter Seven: Anger

In order for you to use your anger constructively, you need to first take an inward look at yourself and ask, *What's wrong in me that needs to be changed?* Whereas God's anger is always righteous, your anger is not always righteous. When God becomes angry, the problem always lies within the world, never within Himself; but when you become angry, sometimes the problem lies within yourself.

When you feel the emotion of anger, view it simply as a red light. It means that something in the world around you or within you is less than what God created it to be; and because you are sinful, you need to be sure that your anger is not caused by your sin.

Years ago I was playing golf with another minister who brought along a friend who supposedly was a good golfer. But on this particular day, the guy wasn't playing well. He hit many double and triple bogies.

About halfway through the course, we reached a par-four hole. His ball was in the fairway. He missed the shot to the green and plopped the ball into a lake. Already angry, he became angrier. He dropped another ball onto the fairway, said a few words, and hit that ball right into the lake, too. Now he became explosive. He dropped a third ball and drove it right into the lake. His anger turned to rage. No, he didn't just throw a golf club. He picked up his entire bag of golf clubs, threw it into the lake, and stalked off the course.

What was wrong? Was it his golf swing? Was it the golf course? Perhaps it was both. But above all, what was wrong existed within himself.

We can all understand his angry reaction; for if we're honest with ourselves, we too have become angry in similar situations. But if we desire to use our righteous anger constructively, we need to examine ourselves. Sometimes our anger is caused by jealousy. Sometimes our anger is caused by prejudice in our hearts. Sometimes our anger is caused by guilt. Sometimes our anger is caused by pride. When our anger is caused by sin, we need to confess our sin and ask God to make us more like Himself.

One day I read about a woman whose husband had an affair. She became enraged. Her self-esteem was deeply wounded. She felt betrayed and rejected. What made the situation even worse is that her husband had the affair with her best friend.

Her husband approached her in a spirit of repentance. "I'll never have an affair again," he promised, "and I've never had one before. Please forgive me. I want to work this out."

Her friend also came to her saying, "I know you may never forgive me, and I don't think I'll ever be able to forgive myself, but please try to forgive me."

A corner of the wife's heart wanted to forgive her husband and her best friend, but she was experiencing so much anger that she couldn't forgive. She asked her minister what to do.

"Overcome evil with good," he responded, simply quoting the Bible. He knew that the Holy Spirit's power would be released in and through her when she began to express love. Go to your husband and your best friend, and begin to do good things for them," he expained.

"Okay," she answered. "I'll do it." She asked the Lord to help her forgive and to overcome her anger. She prayed that the Lord would bless her friend; and even though she didn't feel like it, she began to do acts of kindness for her friend. By the power of God's Spirit, a miracle happened. Her heart was transformed. Her anger waned and then left completely. Love and forgiveness flooded her heart.

She then applied the same biblical formula toward her husband. The process was much harder and took longer, but again a miracle happened. The Lord used her kind actions toward him to remove the anger from her heart and to allow marital reconciliation to occur.

The secular world will not understand stories like this, for they don't make sense without first knowing God and understanding how His healing power works. The secular world says, "Don't get mad, get even." The secular world says, "Get back at the person who wounds you." Yet throughout scripture, God tells us the opposite:

If your enemy is hungry, feed him; if he is thirsty, give
him something to drink.

Proverbs 25:21, Romans 12:20

But I tell you: Love your enemies and pray for those
who persecute you.

Mathew 5:44

Do not take revenge, my friends, but leave room for
God's wrath, for it is written: 'It is mine to avenge; I
will repay'

Romans 12:19, Deuteronomy 32:35

This is a message from God if we are willing to accept it. If we
want to overcome our anger toward another person, we can. We can
perform acts of love for that person through the power of the Holy Spirit.
We shouldn't suppress our anger or vent it. We can overcome it with
good.

Virtue

ℱaith

CHAPTER EIGHT

If its walls could speak, Westminster Abbey would dazzle young and old alike with original stories. All the English rulers from the days of William the Conqueror, except Edward V and Edward VIII, were crowned there. In Britain today there is no greater honor in death than to be buried in Westminster Abbey. Within the boundaries of this famous, thirteenth-century church (officially known as the Collegiate Church of St. Peter), renowned poets, political giants, kings, and queens in British history are buried. It is literally a hall of fame for men and women whom the British esteem highly.

But where is the list of people whom God esteems highly? Which men and women are recorded in His hall of fame? We find their names in Hebrews 11 where we read of Abraham, Sarah, Rahab, David, and many others. And why are these men and women considered great in God's sight? Biblically, the answer is clear. God highly esteemed them because they demonstrated faith. In His sight faith is a cardinal virtue.

Faith Is Greater Than Works

Many of us are familiar with Ephesians 2:8-9: "For it is by grace you have been saved, through faith — and this not from yourselves, it is the gift of God — not by works, so that no one can boast." When the topic of salvation is mentioned, the Bible is clear: Faith is greater than works.

Vice & Virtue: The Battle Within

Millions of people in our world today desperately need to hear this message. Among them are the more than 450 million Hindus. No eastern religion has impacted the western world more than Hinduism has. The New Age Movement is built on Hindu teachings, yet many of us in the western world still do not really understand the Hindu doctrine of salvation.

According to Hindu teaching, there are seven heavens. All are places of reward and pleasure. Above these seven heavens is Moksha, the state in which the soul enters a new level of existence from which it never returns. Beneath these heavens is the earth. Lower still are the seven netherworlds where the demons live. Even lower than these are as many as 8,400,000 hells — plenty of punishment and suffering for everybody. In one hell Hindus believe that birds devour people's flesh year after year. In another hell people are forced to eat a diet of spit, feces, and urine. With this many hells and so few heavens, in Hindu thinking the human condition is indeed tragic.

Who decides whether a Hindu goes to one of the seven heavens or one of the hells? Brahmin does, through a green creature named Yama. Yama wears a red robe, has a flower in his hair, rides a buffalo, and carries a lasso. On what basis does Brahmin or Yama decide whether a Hindu goes to one of the heavens or one of the hells? In Hinduism the answer is clear. The decision is based on the person's karma. Good karma is a result of good works. Bad karma is a result of bad works.

Interestingly, Hinduism reveals that whichever heaven or hell people initally go to, they won't stay there for a long time. Why? The heavens and the hells are temporary stations of reward and pleasure or of punishment and suffering. Eventually, Hindus believe that they all will be sent back to earth through reincarnation so that they might live other lifetimes and have the almost never-ending opportunity to improve their karma. Hindus destined for one of the seven heavens will return to earth as human beings. Hindus destined for one of the hells will return to earth as human beings but only as "untouchables." Hindus who have been really bad may return to earth as animals, insects, or even plants! Furthermore, only after living a number of lifetimes will Hindu followers obtain enough karma to deserve Moksha. Clearly, Hindus hope that through hundreds and perhaps thousands of lifetimes, their karma will improve enough to deserve Moksha. Therefore, when they finally do reach the heaven high above the heavens, they believe they have *earned* it.

Apart from Christianity, all the religions of the world teach the same doctrine: a person is saved by his or her works. That's true of Islam. That's true of Buddhism. That's true of Confucianism. Why? All the religions of the world founded by men reflect human thinking. The founders believed that people must earn the right to go to heaven through works. Even agnostics believe this. Although they are not sure whether heaven exists, they hope that if there is one that they'll be good enough to enter. Why have men and women through the ages consistently believed that they deserve to enter heaven? According to the Bible, pride makes people believe that their good works earn them the right to enter heaven.

The Bible, however, flatly contradicts this doctrine of works. God says we are not good enough to enter heaven. If we each lived a trillion lifetimes, our works would never be good enough to earn and to merit the opportunity to enter heaven and to receive eternal life. The Bible reveals that if we really want to enter heaven, we need to humble ourselves and put our faith in Jesus Christ who died for us. If in faith we embrace Him as our Lord and Savior, He will impute His righteousness to us. He will forgive our sins and will give us the gift of eternal life in heaven. "For it is by grace" — a gift, unmerited favor — that we have been saved "through faith" — faith in Jesus Christ (Ephesians 2:8).

How much faith do you need in order to become a Christian? How much faith do you need in order to obtain the promise of heaven and eternal life? The Bible reveals that you can have some doubts but that you must have enough faith to say, "Lord Jesus, come into my heart. I want to live for You." You must have enough faith to confess that you are sinful and to trust Jesus as your Savior. You must have enough faith to commit your life to His lordship. "For God," according to John 3:16, "so loved the world that he gave his one and only Son, that whoever believes in him shall not perish but have eternal life." Faith in God triumphs over our works.

Faith Is Greater Than Circumstances

No matter what circumstances you may be facing, faith in Jesus Christ is greater than those circumstances. Jesus said,

> If you have faith as small as a mustard seed, you can say to this mountain, 'Move from here to there' and it will move. Nothing will be impossible for you.
>
> Matthew 17:21

You may be facing insurmountable mountains, menacing obstacles, and difficult circumstances in life. Christ, however, is greater than all of them. Through faith in Him, you can gain victory, no matter what your circumstances may be.

Some time ago I read a newspaper article about a young blind girl who was trapped by a raging fire in a New York City apartment. Trapped on the fourth floor, she felt her way onto a window ledge. Smoke and flames billowed all around her. As the building neared collapse, the firefighters placed a net below her and begged her to jump. Fearful, she refused. Panicked, the firefighters called out to her again, but she would not move. Finally, the girl's father arrived. Through a loudspeaker, he called to his daughter and assured her, "Dear, you need to jump, and it's going to be okay. The net is there, and it will hold you. When I count to three, I want you to jump. One, two, three," he counted. She jumped and survived.

Let's reflect on that situation. That little girl faced horrible circumstances. The apartment in which she lived was about to collapse.

Heat seared her skin. She couldn't see. Yet her faith in her father enabled her to overcome her fear. She expressed her faith in her actions.

The same truth applies to those of us who are Christians. No matter how challenging our circumstances may be, only our faith in our Father will bring us through. The apostle Paul faced difficulties much more daunting than most of us will ever face. (See 2 Corinthians 11:23-28). He wrote,"We live by faith, not by sight" (2 Corinthians 5:7). We will all encounter problems, but our faith in Jesus Christ will help us overcome these adverse challenges.

When we look at the people God has listed in Hebrews 11, it's obvious that these heroes of faith were men and women who faced uncertainties and often horrible circumstances.

- Noah lived in a world facing God's judgment. In righteous indignation and heartfelt pain, God was about to bring a flood upon the ungodly world. But because of Noah's obedient faith in God, which he put into action, he and his family were saved (Genesis 6-8).

- Abraham faced an uncertain future when God said to him, "Leave your country, your people and your father's household and go to the land I will show you" (Genesis 12:1). With only God's promises before him, seventy-five-year-old Abraham acted in faith and left Ur of the Chaldeans (Genesis 12). As it turned out, God fulfilled His promises and greatly blessed Abraham. By faith his barren wife Sarah conceived and gave birth to Isaac (Genesis 15, 21).

- In faith Moses refused to be known as the son of Pharaoh's daughter. Although he fled Egypt for forty years, he returned to confront Pharaoh (Exodus 4); and then he led the Israelites out of Egyptian bondage and through the Red Sea (Exodus 14).

• In faith Rahab sheltered two of Joshua's spies in the walled city of Jericho and risked the wrath of the king of Jericho when she helped the spies escape. Because of her faith, she and her entire family were not killed when God enabled the Israelites to conquer Jericho (Joshua 6).

• Gideon, Jephthah, Barak, and Samson each faced vastly superior armies of enemies, yet in faith they obeyed God and won great victories. (See the Book of Judges.)

In fact, as we read in Hebrews 11:33-34, men and women of God "through faith conquered kingdoms, administered justice, and gained what was promised." They also closed lions' mouths, quenched raging fires, and escaped "the edge of the sword." By faith their "weakness was turned to strength." People were resurrected. Formerly weak people became powerful warriors.

What difficult circumstances are you facing today? Maybe you are experiencing financial problems and need to be reminded of Jesus' words:

> Do not worry about your life, what you will eat or drink; or about your body, what you will wear. Is not life more important than food, and the body more important than clothes? . . . And why do you worry about clothes? See how the lilies of the field grow. They do not labor or spin. Yet I tell you that not even Solomon in all his splendor was dressed like one of these. If that is how God clothes the grass of the field, which is here today and tomorrow is thrown into the fire, will he not much more clothe you, O you of little faith?
>
> Matthew 6:25, 28-30

Chapter Eight: Faith

Maybe you are having problems in a relationship. Maybe you are facing medical problems. Maybe you are a single person and would really like to be married someday but feel that there is not a godly man or godly woman for you in this crazy, fallen, mixed-up world. Whatever your circumstances may be, God calls you to act in faith.

In Romans 8:28 Paul wrote, "And we know that in all things God works for the good of those who love him, who have been called according to his purpose." Do you believe that? It takes faith to believe that "in all things God works for the good of those who love him."

I heard a parable about an ant that wanted to cross a concrete slab in order to reach her loved ones living in the ant colony on the other side.

The only way you can cross the slab," she was told, "is to carry this large piece of straw." The straw was quite long and weighed twenty-five times her weight. Still she picked it up and started walking.

As she walked, the straw burdened her greatly. She began to feel bitter. *This is so unfair and unjust,* she thought. *I'm so tired, and this straw is so heavy. Why should I have to carry this?*

About halfway across the slab, she came to a large crack that went from one end of the slab to the other end. No matter how much she stretched, she couldn't span the gap. She looked inside the deep canyon and saw water in the bottom. *What can I do?* she wondered.

Then she made a dramatic discovery. She removed the straw from her back and positioned it in such a way that it spanned the gap. Using it as a bridge, she crossed over and soon rejoined her loved ones.

Although this is just a parable, it illustrates a key truth. Often what we believe to be a burden can really lead to a blessing. Just as the ant's faith in carrying the burden of straw enabled her to travel where she really wanted to go, our willingness to step out in godly faith, despite challenging circumstances, will lead to blessings, if not here on earth, in heaven. If we have faith, God wants us to know that He is able by His power to turn what we believe to be burdens into blessings. But we have to let Him.

Have you ever put together a thousand or five thousand piece puzzle? If you have, you know that unless you look at the picture on the box of the puzzle, the pieces of the puzzle won't make much sense. Without the picture, it is very frustrating to put the puzzle together.

There's a parallel here to our lives. God wants us to know that through faith the pieces of our lives will all come together to make a wonderful picture. Remember that He can see the entire, beautiful picture. Yes, He sometimes allows us to see some of the pieces; but if we are struggling to see the entire picture of our lives, we'll become frustrated. We need to have faith in God, for He truly will work all things together "for the good of those who love him, who have been called according to his purpose" (Romans 8:28). It doesn't matter what our circumstances are.

Even when we are nearing the end of our lives, physical death is just one piece of the puzzle; and God wants us to know that all will be okay. This truth hit home when my next-door neighbor was dying. She was only forty-one years old. Cancer had invaded her body. It went into remission and then returned with a vengeance. She wanted to die at home. Battling her illness was tough, but through it all she and her husband maintained great faith in Christ. Her husband put a little mattress by her bed and stayed by her side nearly twenty-four hours a day. Was it hard to see his beloved wife and friend slip away? You bet! But his faith in Jesus Christ gave him strength to carry on. He knew that she'd be going to heaven, for Jesus promised,

Chapter Eight: Faith

> I am the resurrection and the life. He who believes
> in me will live, even though he dies; and whoever
> lives and believes in me will never die.
>
> John 11:25-26

Shortly before she died, I sat by her bed and talked with her and her husband. Although she was quite weak, she whispered that she wanted to say Psalm 23 aloud with me. We recited the verses, and then I prayed. As I left her room, she said, "I'll see you again." I knew she was referring to seeing me in heaven. In the midst of her circumstances, her faith in Christ was much greater than her fear of physical death.

The apostle Paul stated with confidence,

> For I am convinced that neither death nor life, neither
> angels nor demons, neither the present nor the future,
> nor any powers, neither height nor depth, nor
> anything else in all creation, will be able to separate
> us from the love of God that is in Christ Jesus our
> Lord.
>
> Romans 8:38-39

Because of your faith in God, you can overcome adverse circumstances—even those circumstances that lead to physical death. Your faith is greater than your works. Are you willing to live by faith?

Hope

CHAPTER NINE

On May 13, 1939, nearly two thousand German-Jewish refugees in Germany joyfully boarded a ship named the S. S. St. Louis. They had paid a great deal of money for their tickets. For some it was their entire life savings, but they believed it was well worth the price to escape Nazi persecution. En route to Cuba, they would be able to keep their families together. They would be able to start new lives in a new country. They would have freedom. Their hopes were high.

They weren't aware, however, of one key fact. Adolph Hitler had already arranged another plan. When the ship arrived in Cuba, the refugees were not allowed to emigrate. Their hopes were dashed. In desperation they turned to the United States for help, but for various reasons they were not allowed to emigrate there either. Finally, Captain Gustav Schroeder steered the ship back toward Germany.

Overwhelmed by hopelessness and aware of the suffering that lay ahead, many of the Jews committed suicide during the return voyage. Some of them unsuccessfully attempted to mutiny. Those who were returned to Germany were placed in concentration camps, and many were incinerated in Nazi ovens. Years later a movie titled *Voyage of the Damned* chronicled these Jews' ill-fated voyage. In a sense this tragic story provides a snapshot of what life is like in this world apart from Jesus Christ.

We are all born with hope. When we were young, most of us possessed high hopes of what the day would bring, of what a vacation would be like, or of what we would become when we grew up. But as we have grown older, we have discovered that this life provides more than a little bit of pain and suffering. We have discovered that physical death is inevitable and prearranged; and for some, hopelessness has settled in.

But God doesn't want any of us to be without hope. He wants every man, woman, boy, and girl to have what the Bible calls "living hope." Each of us needs hope in order to live an abundant life. Let's focus on three biblical instructions that God gives us concerning hope.

We Are to Set Our Hope

The apostle Peter wrote,

> Therefore, prepare your minds for action; be self-controlled; *set your hope* fully on the grace to be given you when Jesus Christ is revealed.
>
> 1 Peter 1:13, italics added

Each of us has hope, but we do not all place our hope in the same thing. We each choose in what or in whom we will place our hope. While we set our hope as we choose, God wants us to set our hope wisely. He knows that if we don't our hope will lead to despair and will be in vain.

Do you remember this nursery rhyme? "Ring around the rosy, a pocketful of posies. Ashes, ashes,we all fall down." I remember singing this rhyme when I attended kindergarten at Montrose Elementary School in southern California; and I, like most children (and most adults), didn't know what the words meant. I have come to learn that they describe a time in the Middle Ages when the bubonic plague, the black death, swept across Asia and Europe killing about forty million Europeans between 1347 and 1400. At that time Europeans understandably lived in panic, chaos, and fear. Medical knowledge was primitive, and people didn't know what was causing the plague. They only knew that people were dying all around them.

Suspecting that polluted air was the cause, many people tried various methods to ward off the plague. Historians reveal that many family members entered public rose gardens, held hands, and then circled the rose bushes believing that as they breathed in the fragrances they would purify the polluted air in their lungs. People also placed the petals from posies into their pockets. From time to time during the day, these people removed a petal and smelled it, again trying to purify the air they breathed in order to ward off this black death. Another common method involved putting ashes in spoons and then inhaling the ashes in order to induce sneezing. When people sneezed, they believed that the polluted air was thrown out of their nasal passages and lungs.

In the end, however, all the people fell down; and laborers in the streets of London repeated the chant as they picked up the dead bodies of plague victims. Sadly, those who became victims of the black plague set their hopes wrongly on "rosies," posies, and ashes.

Have you read the *Humanist Manifestos One* and *Two*? Many secular humanists view these documents as their bible. I have read these documents; and I marvel that some of the most brilliant men and women in America, leaders of political parties and educators from some of the finest academic institutions, have signed them.

Secular humanists do not believe in God. Instead they place all their hopes in mankind, believing that the hope of this world lies in people. Secular humanists believe that through evolution and technology mankind will usher in a golden age in which disease, war, and pestilence will be eradicated from the earth and peace will flood the earth like a sea. Secular humanists view people as highly evolved animals who, through millions of years of cell mutation and natural selection, have evolved from hairy quadrupeds into modern, shoe-shined, hair-combed bipeds. Modern man is still evolving; and even though secular humanists don't know what modern man will ultimately become, they believe in man's ultimate ascendancy.

Secular humanists also believe in social Darwinism, that human society is evolving toward perfection. Yet we see that moral and ethical values are eroding. We see that more people have been killed in wars during the twentieth century than during any previous century. We still see deep hatred and selfishness exhibited in people's hearts. Human society is not gloriously improving.

Furthermore, although technology has brought us miracle cures in medicine, it has also brought us the atomic bomb and germ warfare. Truly, as Aleksandr Solzhenitsyn says,

> All the glorified technological attainments of the twentieth century cannot begin to redeem us of our moral poverty. Given the depravity of the human heart, it is more likely that technology will ultimately destroy us instead of save us.

The theories of evolution, social Darwinism, and technology resemble "rosies," posies, and ashes. The theory of evolution offers no genuine hope and is filled with inexplicable gaps, wrong assumptions, and greatly manipulated data. According to the second law of thermodynamics, our physical universe is winding down. It's not progressing toward perfection. It's moving toward randomness, disorder, and chaos.

Instead of obtaining hope through secular humanism, some people have chosen to set their hopes on materialism, hedonism, or, what I label, ascensionism—climbing the so-called ladder of success. *If somewhere down the road I can just get enough money and accumulate enough possessions, I'll be happy and content. If I can just get enough pleasure out of life, I'll find fulfillment. If I can climb the ladder of success and obtain power, position, prestige, and prominence, I'll be content.*

But past and unfolding history reveal that materialism, hedonism, and ascensionism are just a different form of "rosies," posies, and ashes. They are what the Bible labels vanity, "a chasing after the wind" (Ecclesiastes 1:14, 17), and they offer no genuine hope. People who pursue such vain hope and who entice other people to do so are what the apostle Peter calls "springs without water and mists driven by a storm" (2 Peter 2:17).

The Bible clearly states that if we really want a future that isn't founded on vanity or that doesn't end in despair we must set our hope on Jesus Christ and His promises. We must set our hope "fully on the grace to be given [us] when Jesus Christ is revealed" (1 Peter 1:13). We must set our hope on His grace, on His person, and on His promises. Nothing else is worthy of our pursuit. All else is vanity.

We Are to Take Hold of the Hope Set Before Us

The Cape of Good Hope is a peninsula about one hundred miles northwest of the southernmost tip of Africa. Today the peninsula is known for its fine roads and sandy beaches, but years ago people held a different view. According to tradition, the peninsula was first sighted in 1488 by the Portuguese navigator Bartholomeu Dias, who called it the Cape of Storms because that's all he found there.

Later King John II of Portugal renamed it the Cape of Good Hope because he believed its discovery was a good omen that anyone who sailed around the peninsula from Europe would ultimately reach the glory of India. People mocked the king for his hope, saying, in effect, "No. If you continue on, you'll only find an endless sea, or maybe the world will just drop off and take you with it." But the king stood firm in his belief.

In November 1497, another Portuguese explorer named Vasco da Gama took hold of the hope. Joining with sailors of like mind and like hope, he put his life on the line. In commitment and faith, he and the crew sailed around the Cape of Good Hope and continued on until they reached Calicut, India, in May 1498. Hope became fact.

God wants us to realize that it's not enough just to set our hope. We have to take hold of the hope with the faith of commitment.

Vice & Virtue: The Battle Within

> We who have fled *to take hold of the hope* offered to
> us may be greatly encouraged. We have this hope
> as an anchor for the soul, firm and secure.
>
> Hebrews 6:18b,19a, italics added

The Greek word *krateo* used in verse 18 literally means "to grab hold." As we read elsewhere in Hebrews 6, God set His promises before Abraham. But in order to take hold of that hope, Abraham needed the active faith of commitment, not merely the faith of mere intellectual assent. He needed the patient endurance of commitment, not the patience of passivity. You see, he had to leave his home in Ur of the Chaldeans and live in the land of promise in tents. Later he had to be willing to offer up his only son in faith. Through active faith and commitment, he took hold of the hope of God's promises.

In whom or in what do you set your hope? If you claim to have set your hope in Christ and in His promises, you need to take hold of that hope through a faith that expresses itself through active, daily commitment and patient endurance. Nothing else will work. Nothing else will satisfy. If you don't take hold of the hope, your hope will be in vain.

Pollsters, who regularly take the religious pulse of the American people, reveal that most people in the United States claim to believe in the deity of Christ and in the infallible authority of the Bible. According to these polls, most Americans also claim to believe in heaven and have set their hopes on being there one day. These claims amaze me because so many Americans are not willing to take hold of this hope through the faith of commitment. In fact, according to pollster George Gallup, we are a nation built on religious hypocrisy. According to his polls, most people in the United States are not willing to live their lives in conformity to the teachings of Christ nor even to read His teachings in the Bible.

Don't let that be true of you. If you really believe in Christ, take hold of the hope He offers. Live for Him day by day. Honor Him in everything you think and do.

Chapter Nine: Hope

Do you really want to go to heaven? Is that your hope? If so, you need to put your personal faith in Christ and live for Him, your Lord and Savior. Nothing less will be sufficient.

Do you really want to improve your life and the lives of other people you love? Is that your hope? If so, you need to be committed to prayer because the Bible reveals that prayer changes lives and situations.

Do you really want all things to work together for good in your life (Romans 8:28)? Then you need to love God with all your heart, soul, and mind.

Do you really want God to open up the windows of heaven for you and to pour down on you an overflowing blessing? Then you need to demonstrate your commitment by tithing.

> 'Bring the whole tithe into the storehouse that there may be food in my house. Test me in this,' says the Lord Almighty, 'and see if I will not throw open the floodgates of heaven and pour out so much blessing that you will not have room enough for it.'
>
> Malachi 3:10

Take hold of the hope set before you. Commit yourself to love and to obey God.

We Are to Share Our Hope With Others

God also calls us to offer the hope we have in Jesus Christ to other people. Each of us can give some measure of hope to another person. In 1 Peter 3:15, the apostle Peter wrote, "Always be prepared to give an answer to everyone who asks you to give the reason for the hope that you have."

In 1875, just outside Boston, a half blind nine-year-old orphan lived in an institution for the criminally insane. The workers in the institution named her Little Annie. They believed she was hopelessly insane because when people came near her, she would either completely ignore them or become enraged and attack them. Not knowing what else to do with her, they placed Little Annie in a cage in the basement of the institution where she wouldn't see any people.

An elderly Christian nurse, however, had a sense of hope for Little Annie and prayed for her. Every day this nurse went into the basement dungeon and ate her lunch by the little girl's cage. Little Annie didn't seem to notice her sitting there. Later the nurse began bringing in cookies or brownies she had baked and would leave them by Little Annie's cage. Sure enough, when the nurse came back, the cookies or brownies were gone.

The nurse continued to pray for Little Annie; and as time passed, the young girl responded, regained hope, and communicated with the elderly nurse. Other staff workers began noticing the changes in Little Annie, and they eventually moved her upstairs. She continued to improve. By 1880, she was allowed to leave the institution; but she asked to stay so that she could help others.

Little Annie's hope grew. In 1881, she underwent surgery at the Perkins Institute for the Blind in Boston to restore some of her sight. In 1887, then twenty-one years old, Annie underwent a second surgery; more of her sight was restored.

That same year in Alabama lived a seven-year-old girl who was blind, deaf, and mute — completely separated from the world due to a brain fever illness she suffered when she was eighteen months old. She lived in her own inner dungeon with thoughts that only she knew. Hopelessness invaded her life. Her name? Helen Keller.

Although friends of Helen Keller couldn't communicate with her, they cared about her. A doctor urged Helen's father to consult with Alexander Graham Bell, who had invented the telephone. They did, and Bell directed them to write to the Perkins Institute for the Blind to inquire about a young woman named Anne Sullivan — Little Annie. Bell believed that Anne would be able to help Helen.

On March 3, 1887, Anne Sullivan traveled to Alabama to work with Helen Keller. In two weeks, through touch, she had taught Helen thirty words. Over the next forty-nine years, Anne remained by Helen's side. She taught Helen to read Braille. She taught Helen how to speak. From 1896 to 1900, she sat with Helen in every class at the Cambridge School for Young Ladies. She assisted Helen in her studies at Radcliffe College, where Helen graduated *cum laude* in 1904. She inspired Helen with hope to write books.

When Anne died in 1936, Helen said, "I pray that God will give me courage to face the silent dark until she smiles on me again." Helen had never seen Anne's smile, but the hope she felt when she was in Anne's presence felt like a smile. When Helen died in 1968, her burial urn was placed next to Anne's in the National Cathedral in Washington, D.C.

People have asked me if Anne Sullivan and Helen Keller were Christians. That I don't know, but I do know that as Christians we are called to share hope. We are each called to bring spiritual light into the darkness that others experience. No one else can share hope as we can because only we have the Lord of Hope living in our hearts. Will you come alongside another person during his or her moment of darkness and pain and by the power of Christ minister in encouragement?

Over the years I've visited people in hospitals. I've seen some people approach death in sheer terror and utter panic. I've seen other people approach death with hopeless resignation. But as Christians we can approach death with hope, joy, anticipation, and excitement because the Lord of Hope lives in our hearts. He has assured us of His promise of eternal life. Christ's hope is meant to be shared. It's His hope of glory that we are called to share.

The Bible reveals that at one time sin separated all of us from God. We were all alienated from His covenants and promises. Without God, there would be no hope. But now as Christians we have received His grace and mercy so that we might declare the wonderful deeds of the One "who called [us] out of darkness into his wonderful light" (1 Peter 2:9). Once we were on our own, without a true identity. Now as Christians we are a part of God's family. Once we had not received mercy. Now as Christians we have received mercy. (See I Peter 2:10.)

Jesus said, "You are the light of the world" (Matthew 5:14; see also Acts 13:47 and 2 Corinthians 4:6). God calls us to reflect His light in a world of spiritual darkness — a world of disease and infirmity. God calls us to be salt that seasons all that it touches.

God calls us to set our hope on Him and to take hold of His promises. God calls us to take hold of our hope in Christ and to demonstrate it through true faith that expresses itself in daily commitment. God calls us to share that hope with other people through the love and the power of Jesus Christ for His sake. Truly, every other hope is in vain.

$\mathcal{L}$ove

CHAPTER TEN

Picture this scene. The Sadducees, the key religious rulers in Israel, have just failed to trap Jesus by asking him a difficult question. Consequently, a second group of religious rulers, the Pharisees, step in with their question of challenge.

"Teacher," an expert in the religious law asks, "which is the greatest commandment in the Law?" (Matthew 22:36).

Jesus answered,

> 'Love the Lord your God with all your heart and with all your soul and with all your mind.' This is the first and greatest commandment. And the second is like it: 'Love your neighbor as yourself.' All the Law and the Prophets hang on these two commandments.
>
> Matthew 22:37-40

Obviously, God believes that love is *the* cardinal virtue. What is more important to Him than anything else is that you and I love Him with all our hearts, with all our souls, and with all our minds.

Let's say that I am seated across from you right now; and I ask you, "Do you love God?"

Most likely you would quickly answer, "Yes, I love God." (I'd respond the same way if you asked me that question.) According to the Bible, however, many of us misunderstand the biblical concept of loving God. Sometimes we think that we love Him, but our lives fail to reflect that love. Perhaps that's why God gave us two tests in His Word by which we will know that we love Him and by which He will know that we love Him.

Test #1: If We Love God, We Will Obey His Commandments

In the fall of 1038, King Henry III, the king of Germany, wearily placed the body of his beloved Queen Kunagunda into a tomb. Having loved her deeply, he now felt great despair. He wearied of court life. He wearied of the throne. As Jesus Christ was the only person he loved more than he had loved the queen, the king reasoned, *I'll leave the throne and join the monastery. There I'll spend the rest of my life quietly contemplating the glory of God.*

Poor Richard, the priest who led the monastery, knew that King Henry III loved God. Wanting the king to remain on the throne, the priest inquired, "King Henry, do you understand that if you come to this monastery you'll have to take a vow — a vow of total and complete obedience?"

Without hesitating, the king responded, "I understand, and I vow to you that for the rest of my life I will obey your every command as you hear the voice of Christ."

Poor Richard thought for a moment and then said, "Very well. This is my command. Return to the throne. Return to the place where God has placed you and serve Him there with all your heart."

Obediently, the king returned to the throne of Germany where he sought to serve Christ faithfully and to obey Him in all things. God, in turn, blessed him. In 1043, he met Agnes whom he later married. In 1046, he became the Holy Roman Emperor of all Europe. Before his death in 1056, he had appointed four of the popes of Rome, thus appointing more popes than any other king in history. Upon his death these words were inscribed above his tomb: "He learned to rule by obedience to God."

Why did King Henry III long to obey God? Why do historians remember him as a ruler who obeyed God perhaps more than any other earthly ruler to date? The answer is simple. He longed to obey God because He loved God with all his heart, soul, and mind.

Let's look at a few reasons why people obey laws even when they don't want to do so.

Fear

When we think of the role that fear can play in motivating people to obey, rulers such as Attila the Hun, Vlad the Impaler, and Ivan the Terrible may come to mind. These men ruled their kingdoms with iron fists and imposed obedience through reigns of terror. Thus it is easy to think that to obey out of fear is an improper motive. But this isn't necessarily true. After all, history also contains many accounts of good kings and good kingdoms that used fear as a proper motive for obedience. Even in this country fear is used to motivate us to obey laws.

For instance, when you drove to church or to the grocery store this past week, you stopped at stop signs and at red traffic lights. You turned left or right from the appropriate lanes. You stayed within the speed limits—or close to them. Why did you obey those traffic laws? Most likely you obeyed out of fear. If you didn't obey them, you knew that a police officer might pull you over or you might cause an accident.

Fear can be a proper motive; and as seen in 1 Peter 1:14-17, sometimes God uses fear to motivate us.

As obedient children, do not conform to the evil desires you had when you lived in ignorance. But just as he who called you is holy, so be holy in all you do; for it is written: 'Be holy, because I am holy.' Since you call on a Father who judges each man's work impartially, live your lives as strangers here in reverent fear.

In various Scripture passages, God emphasizes that He will judge us. Romans 2:1-16, for example, describes God's righteous judgment and reveals that He will even judge our secrets! 1 Corinthians 10:11 mentions how God punished the Israelites for their disobedience and goes on to explain that "these things happened to them as examples and were written down as warnings for us, on whom the fulfillment of the ages has come." As recorded in Matthew 7:1-2, Jesus said, "Do not judge, or you too will be judged. For in the same way you judge others, you will be judged, and with the measure you use, it will be measured to you."

While it is true that "perfect love drives out fear, because fear has to do with punishment. The one who fears is not made perfect in love" (1 John 4:18), we must face the reality that God would rather have us obey Him out of fear than not to obey Him at all!

Anticipation of Reward

People also obey because they desire to be rewarded. Virtually all the religions of the world offer rewards for obedience. According to the teachings of Mohammed in the Koran, obedient Islamic men will go to Paradise. There they will feast at a three-hundred-course dinner, receive eternal youthfulness, and possess a palace with eighty thousand servants and seventy-two wives. These men are also promised that they can father children by any of their wives and that their children will grow from birth to maturity in just one hour (without the hassles of the teenage years)! Why did Mohammed put these made-up, carnal rewards in the Koran? He knew that he needed to offer the incentive of reward in order to motivate his followers' obedience.

The God of the Bible offers us genuine and beautiful heavenly rewards for our obedience, not carnal rewards. Of course, we do not obtain eternal life in heaven through our obedience but only by placing our personal faith in Jesus Christ. When those of us who have placed our faith in Him die physically, we will receive varying heavenly rewards according to our faithfulness and obedience to Him here on earth. In 1 Samuel 26:23, David said, "The Lord rewards every man for his righteousness and faithfulness." Jesus spoke of eternal rewards in Matthew 5:11-12.

> Blessed are you when people insult you, persecute you and falsely say all kinds of evil against you because of me. Rejoice and be glad, because great is your reward in heaven.
>
> See also Matthew 6:1-18; 10:41-42.

The Bible also makes it clear that God will give us earthly rewards for our obedience.

> Blessed is the man, who does not walk in the counsel of the wicked or stand in the way of sinners or sit in the seat of mockers. But his delight is in the law of the Lord, and on his law he meditates day and night. He is like a tree planted by streams of water, which yields its fruit in season and whose leaf does not wither. Whatever he does prospers.
>
> Psalm 1:1-3

> Honor the LORD with your wealth, with the firstfruits of all your crops; then your barns will be filled to overflowing, and your vats will brim over with new wine.
>
> Proverbs 3:9,10

Love

Love is a much better motivator for obedience than fear and reward. We might recall Jesus' challenging words to His disciples: "If you love me, you will obey what I command" (John 14:15). A moment later Jesus added, "Whoever has my commands and obeys them, he is the one who loves me. . . . He who does not love me will not obey my teaching" (John 14:21, 24).

Although more and more people today claim to love God, Judeo-Christian values are eroding. The commands of God as given in Holy Scripture are being greatly violated in our generation and culture. How can this be? Simply, many people want to do as they please. They say they love God, but they don't want to obey Him.

The biblical message is clear. If we love God, we will keep His commandments: "This is love for God: to obey his commands" (1 John 5:3). We will desire to please Him, to honor Him, and to obey Him. We will strive with all our hearts to obey Him, no matter how difficult that may be or how fallen the world around us may be.

God is most pleased when our obedience to Him is rooted in agape love. The Greek word *agape* originally meant "to honor." Thus if we love God, we will honor Him by chosing to obey Him. That's why Jesus said that if we love Him, we will keep His commandments. Thus if we don't keep God's commandments, we really don't love Him.

Sadly, some people do keep God's commandments, but they do not love Him. The Scribes and the Pharisees, for example, obeyed many of God's commandments; but they did so out of pride and self-righteousness. They obeyed God's commandments to please and to exalt themselves, not to please and to exalt God. It would have been far better for those religious rulers if they had obeyed God out of godly fear, reverence, and awe. It would have been far better if they had obeyed God because they desired the eternal rewards only He can give. It would have been best for them, however, if they had obeyed God out of love for Him.

If you are a parent, you probably understand what it means to obey out of love. My wife Barbara and I have two children, Heather and Drew. As we instructed them through the years, sometimes their obedience was rooted in fear and the knowledge that we would discipline them if they didn't obey. Sometimes their obedience was rooted in rewards, which we at times used as incentives. But what pleased us most, as their mother and father, was when they obeyed us out of love because they wanted to honor and to please us. God feels like that, too. He wants our love for Him to be the underlying motive for our obedience.

Test #2: If We Love God, We Will Love People

If we love God, we will not only obey His commandments, but also we will love people. I've heard many people say, "I love God. It's people I can't stand." Sometimes we all feel like that; but the reality is that if we really love God, we will have His heart for people. We will want to help them. We will love them. John, the beloved disciple of Jesus, wrote:

> Anyone who claims to be in the light but hates his brother is still in the darkness. Whoever loves his brother lives in the light, and there is nothing in him to make him stumble.... If anyone says, "I love God," yet hates his brother, he is a liar. For anyone who does not love his brother, whom he has seen, cannot love God, whom he has not seen. And he has given us this command: Whoever loves God must also love his brother.
>
> 1 John 2:9-10; 4:20-21

As mentioned, in Matthew 22:37-39, Jesus said to the Pharisees, " 'Love the Lord your God with all your heart and with all your soul and with all your mind.' This is the first and greatest commandment." But then a second commandment immediately followed. "And the second is like it: 'Love your neighbor as yourself.' "

Our Family

If we really love God, we will love people—beginning with our families. In this fallen world, in which there is so much suffering and rejection, it's tough for each of us to make it through life without the loving support of some kind of family.

Bart Starr played for the Green Bay Packers. Some people say that he was one of the greatest National Football League quarterbacks. During the 1966 football season, his son Bart, Jr. was struggling academically. Bart, Sr. said, "Son, for every perfect paper you get, I'll give you a dime." (Today a dime doesn't seem like much money, but back then it had fairly good purchasing power.) His son became motivated to improve his schoolwork.

That same year the Green Bay Packers played the St. Louis Cardinals in St. Louis. The game was aired on national television, and Bart, Sr. played one of the worst games of his life. He couldn't hold onto the football. He couldn't throw the ball, and he couldn't connect with his receivers. As a result, the St. Louis Cardinals annihilated his team.

During the flight home, Bart, Sr. felt humiliated. He felt like a loser. But when he walked into his bedroom about midnight, a note on his pillow caught his eye. It was from his son who had written, "Dear Dad: I watched the game tonight. I thought you were great. Dad, I love you. Bart, Jr." Taped to the note were two dimes.

What happened between that father and son needs to happen in our families today. We need to love the members of our families. We need to support each other and stay together even when times are tough.

As Christians the love that we express to our families is meant to be even greater than the love that secular people without God can offer. God commands, "Husbands, love your wives, just as Christ loved the church and gave himself up for her to make her holy" (Ephesians 5:25-26). What a powerful challenge! Husbands are to love their wives in the same way that Jesus sacrificially gave His life for the Church! That's agape love, and we are to express this love to our families first.

Other Christians

We are also to extend our godly love to people outside our immediate families. We are to extend the loving heart of God to the

Church. God commands us to love our brothers and sisters in Christ. The apostle Peter wrote, "Show proper respect to everyone: Love the brotherhood of believers . . ." (1 Peter 2:17).

This is not always easy, for many Christians aren't easy to love. Some Christians use their faith to manipulate in business. Some Christians are self-righteous and narrow-minded in their judgments of others. Some Christians are self-centered and extremely hard to get along with. Yet Christ calls us to love them for they are brothers and sisters in Christ.

On January 23, 1968, the North Koreans captured the United States intelligence-gathering ship Pueblo off the coast of North Korea. Eighty-three American officers and crewmen were captured and then abused. As part of their torture, thirteen men were selected to sit in thirteen chairs, each chair having a different number. Each man was ordered to sit for hours, without moving, in the same chair each day.

On the first day, in front of the other men, the North Koreans beat and flogged the man sitting in chair "1." The captors then explained that they would continue to do this everyday until this man died. True to their word, the second and third day the North Koreans continued their brutality, beating the same man in chair "1" while the other twelve men watched.

But on the fourth day the North Koreans were amazed to see that another man from the group was voluntarily sitting in chair "1" and ready to be beaten. Therefore, they beat the volunteer. The next day the North Koreans found yet another man sitting in chair "1" and beat him. This happened day after day as the thirteen men voluntarily rotated. After a while, the North Koreans became so frustrated that they stopped their beatings.

These thirteen men demonstrated a love that bound them. They willingly supported each other in the midst of great persecution as together they shared the afflictions of the man in chair "1." Their love for one another ultimately enabled them to survive and not to be conquered by their common enemy.

This example of love gives those of us who are Christians insight into an even greater kind of love that we are to demonstrate—the love of Christ in us. We, too, face an enemy—Satan and his spiritual forces. (See Ephesians 6.) He seeks to destroy us. He seeks to break up our unity. He seeks to make us self-centered and to take our focus off our brothers and sisters. He seeks not only to remove the joy of our salvation in Christ but also to make us unwilling to bond together and to share each others' afflictions and joys.

In fact, the Bible reveals that only as we Christians love each other will the non-Christian world be drawn to the Gospel of Jesus Christ. The secular world is supposed to look at the Church and exclaim, "Wow! These Christians sure demonstrate love to one another." When we love each other, non-Christians will be drawn to Christ like iron is drawn to a magnet.

Our Neighbors

God commands us to love our families and other Christians. He also commands us to love our "neighbors"—a category that includes people who have not yet placed their faith in Jesus Christ as well as those in need.

During the summer of 1928, in Massachusetts, a young man walked onto an ocean pier, tripped on a rope, and fell into the water. He didn't know how to swim. He struggled and cried out for help.

At the end of the pier another young man was sitting on a deck chair, sunbathing. An excellent swimmer, he heard the man's cries, but he merely watched as other people from farther away ran down the pier, dove into the water, and tried to rescue the drowning man. Sadly, they did not reach him in time.

The family of the man who drowned sued the young man who remained in the deck chair. After much legal maneuvering, the State of Massachusetts and the United States Government ruled that the man who had remained in the chair had no legal obligation to help the drowning man and could not be held criminally responsible. The United

States courts agreed with Cain who said to God, "Am I my brother's keeper?" (Genesis 4:9).

According to the laws of this world, you and I have no legal obligation to love our neighbors; but if we say we love God, we have a God-given obligation to love our neighbors. The man who remained seated in the deck chair didn't love God. He couldn't have loved God and watched another human being drown without doing something to help. The secular world must see that we not only know the truths of God but also that we live out these truths.

> If anyone has material possessions and sees his brother in need but has no pity on him, how can the love of God be in him?
>
> 1 John 3:17

Jesus calls us to demonstrate a mysterious love so great that it even extends to our enemies! He said,

> But I tell you who hear me: Love your enemies, do good to those who hate you, bless those who curse you, pray for those who mistreat you. . . . If you love those who love you, what credit is that to you? Even 'sinners' love those who love them.
>
> Luke 6:27-28, 32

God calls us to demonstrate a special kind of love. Let us reflect on the following verses and choose today to obey God's commands and to demonstrate the love that Jesus Christ demonstrated for us.

> If I speak in the tongues of men and of angels, but have not love, I am only a resounding gong or a clanging cymbal. If I have the gift of prophecy and can fathom all mysteries and all knowledge, and if I

have a faith that can move mountains, but have not love, I am nothing. If I give all I possess to the poor and surrender my body to the flames, but have not love, I gain nothing. . . . And now these three remain: faith, hope and love. But the greatest of these is love. Follow the way of love.

1 Corinthians 13:1-3, 13; 14:1

Justice

What happens to people after they die? This question has stimulated much debate and controversy, and it continues to do so. Bookstores contain numerous books on the subject. Magazine articles report what people claim they have experienced after they "died" and returned to life. Philosophers and theologians have developed numerous theories about the afterlife. According to the Bible, however, there are only two eternal destinies—heaven or hell.

In today's world many people are concerned about the justice of God. They want to know that God is just. They want to know that His eternal judgments are fair and equitable. The fact that the God of the Bible speaks only of heaven and hell seems too black and white to them and not entirely just. Thus they create their own theories.

Certain liberal theologians, for example, proclaim the doctrine of universalism, which teaches that ultimately everyone will go to heaven and no one will go to hell. This seems just to them. Other theologians believe that the doctrine of annihilation is just. According to this doctrine, wicked people will simply be annihilated and will fade out of existence because it isn't just for even these people to suffer for eternity.

Roman Catholic theologians came up with the doctrine of purgatory because it seemed just to them that most Christians should have to suffer a little bit before entering heaven. These theologians also came up with the doctrine of limbo (from the Latin word *limbus* that means "border" or "between") because it seemed just to them that not everyone should go to heaven or to hell. *Why shouldn't people, they thought, spend eternity in another condition? Babies die in infancy without being baptized. Adults live and die without ever hearing the Gospel of Jesus Christ. Certainly, these people don't qualify for heaven; yet they don't deserve hell.*

No matter what people believe about the afterlife, the Bible teaches that God is completely just. In Revelation 15:3, we read that seven angels will sing "the song of Moses the servant of God and the song of the Lamb: 'Great and marvelous are your deeds, Lord God Almighty. Just and true are your ways, King of the ages.'"

A psalmist, Ethan the Ezrahite praised the character of God and wrote, "Righteousness and justice are the foundation of your throne; love and faithfulness go before you" (Psalm 89:14).

Because God is just, no one has to worry about His justice. Instead we are to focus on our own justice. Consider these words of the prophet Ezekiel:

> Yet you say, 'The way of the Lord is not just.' Hear, O house of Israel: Is my way unjust? Is it not your ways that are unjust?
>
> Ezekiel 18:25

A Just Person Seeks to Live a Righteous Life

The word in the Bible translated "just" or "justice" is the word *dikaios*. This legal term is often translated "righteous" because to the early Christians to be just meant to be righteous and to be righteous meant to obey God's laws. Therefore, in order to be just, a person needed to be obedient to God's laws.

When I think of people throughout the centuries who may or may not have been just, Captain William Kidd comes to mind. His life has become famous through legend. People all over the world have sung a ballad about him, and Robert Louis Stevenson supposedly based the book *Treasure Island* on Kidd's life. But there's much more to his story than you may know.

Born in 1645, in Scotland, Kidd lived in colonial New York City for a while as a respected trader and sea captain.

In 1695, King William III of England commissioned Kidd and gave him the title "Privateer," which entitled him to captain an armed ship representing England. The king mandated that Kidd capture pirates who were plundering English ships.

In 1696, Kidd set sail from London with a hand-picked crew; but a British warship needing crew members soon came by and under English rights removed many of Kidd's crew members. Lacking men, Kidd traveled to New York City and selected crew members from the city's pirate-infested population. In September 1696, he left New York City and attacked two French ships, which he sank. This action was legal because England and France were at war.

Then Kidd traveled to Madagascar and the West Indies where he learned that the English had declared him a pirate. Legend holds that he stopped at an island to bury his treasure before sailing to New York where he claimed his innocence and turned himself over to the authorities. The English took him back to London and charged him with five acts of piracy.

Did Kidd really perform acts of piracy? No one knows but God. We do know that he was not allowed to have legal counsel during his trial. We do know that the evidence he wished to present was deemed inadmissible. We do know that in front of the magistrates of England he continued to say these words: "I am a just man." He believed that he was innocent of disobeying the laws of England. The court, however, declared him guilty; and on May 23, 1701, he was hanged. His body was left to rot near the Thames River in London as a warning to all British citizens to obey British laws.

If you and I were to state the words, "I am a just man in the sight of God" or "I am a just woman in the sight of God" in a fashion similar to Kidd's declaration before the magistrates of England, we would not be saying, "I obey all the laws of my country." Rather we would each be saying, "I obey all the laws of God." Therein lies the problem; for if we disobey even one law of God, we are not just.

The Bible clearly states that no person can become just based on his or her own actions. Paul wrote in Romans 3:23 that "all have sinned and fall short of the glory of God." In Romans 3:19-20, he wrote,

> Now we know that whatever the law says, it says to those who are under the law, so that every mouth may be silenced and the whole world held accountable to God. Therefore no one will be declared righteous in his sight by observing the law; rather, through the law we become conscious of sin.

According to the Bible, none are righteous but one (Psalm 53:1-3; Romans 3:10). Only one man has perfectly obeyed all the laws of God. Only one man can say that he is just. That man is Jesus Christ. "And in him is no sin" (1 John 3:5). Because He perfectly obeyed the laws of God, He satisfied all the demands of justice.

He even paid the penalty for all the sins of every person who has disobeyed God's laws, once again satisfying the demands of God's justice. When He died on the cross and rose again for our sins, "he sacrificed for [our] sins once for all when he offered himself" (Hebrews 7:27). The apostle Paul explained, "God made [Jesus] who had no sin to be sin for us, so that in him we might become the righteousness of God" (2 Corinthians 5:21). That's an amazing truth!

If you are not yet a Christian, take note. If in faith you invite Jesus to become the Lord of your life and your Savior from sin, then you will come under the umbrella of what Jesus accomplished on the cross when He took all the sins of mankind onto Himself. You will be *just*ified. Your sins will be forgiven.

112

Chapter Eleven: Justice

Though your sins are like scarlet, they shall be as white as snow; though they are red as crimson, they shall be like wool.

Isaiah 1:18

In the courtroom of heaven, you will be pronounced just. As God views you through the completed work of His Son and as His Son's righteousness is imputed to you, you will be pronounced innocent. This is the good news of the Gospel. This is the message of the Bible. Truly, "the just shall live by his faith" (Habakkuk 2:4, *The New King James Version*). If you come to Jesus Christ in faith, embracing Him as Lord and Savior, you will become just in the sight of God and will satisfy His laws. You will be declared innocent under God's laws through what Christ has done for you. This is an incredible deal!

Maybe you attend a small church. Maybe you attend a large one. In our church, Cherry Hills Community Church, there are quite a few members, many of whom make a tremendous effort to get to know other members. But there's one member of the church whom virtually none of our congregation knows. He has never attended our church. He has never seen any of our members. Why? Because he's in a federal prison in Mississippi for murder.

This member wrote a letter to our congregation and asked that it be read aloud. I include it here because it's a powerful statement of how Christ can justify any of us.

The reason this is being read to you rather than my being present is because I'm serving a life sentence in the Mississippi Department of Corrections for committing a murder while in a drug-demented state of mind. My story is not a pretty one. Life is often not pretty so I shall share briefly what it was that life unfolded for me.

Vice & Virtue: The Battle Within

I had it all—a fine home, my own television show, nice cars, a wonderful family and friends that few of us are ever privileged enough to enjoy. Yet none of it was enough. There remained a void that could not be filled with any amount of wealth or power or prestige. There was an emptiness that ate like a cancer, slowly eroding my heart, festering a bitterness and an anger that would not, even with the finest the world had to offer, go away. The only time I could even face myself in the mirror was when I was either high on cocaine or stone drunk, so my drinking and my drug abuse became a common occurrence.

Eventually the cocaine abuse got the best of me. Within three months from taking my first bit of cocaine, I sat in a jail cell facing the death sentence for murder.

What is even worse, however, was that I really did want the state to take my life for I was too much of a coward to do it myself. So I waited. On November 7, 1986 while sitting in that jail cell, I decided no longer to wait on the state to carry out what I thought surely would be a speedy justice. At about 2:00 a.m., I got up from the steel cot, retrieved a razor blade I had hidden earlier and decided not to be anymore. God, however, did not see it that way. As I raised the razor [blade] to my wrist, the images of my beautiful daughter shimmered before me. Then in words that were almost audible, I heard, "Is that the way you want Brittany to remember her daddy?" I fell face down on the floor crying and screaming, "I hate you, God. How could you allow this to happen to me?"

114

Somehow in my sick and addicted mind, I blamed God for all that had befallen me. Yet with each tear that fell from my face, I could feel the pain and bitterness dissolving like the dust in a rainstorm. After about twenty minutes of this, I soon found myself saying, "God, I need you. I need you."

God heard my cry and came into my life through Jesus Christ. I was saved—not just from the death penalty, not just from my addictions, not just from myself—but I was saved for all eternity. Since coming to know Christ, He has blessed me in many truly amazing ways.

This man then went on to describe how he had corresponded with Tom Melton (then pastor of congregational life at our church and now senior pastor of Greenwood Community Church in Greenwood Village, Colorado) and how he had become aware that God wanted him to become a member of Cherry Hills Community Church.

At first I argued with God for it seemed like such a silly idea. I mean, after all, I could not attend any of the services and I couldn't meet any of you. I surely had nothing to offer in the way of serving, so what good would it do for me to join? I wrestled with the question and with God for nearly a year before I wrote to Tom and expressed my desire to join. Surprisingly, Tom thought it was a fantastic idea. I thought when I wrote and told him what was on my mind that he would think I was crazy, but apparently God knew what He was doing; and since joining, I've felt more and more like I belong. As funny as this may sound, it was kind of like coming home.

Although I feel good about being a member of the body of believers at Cherry Hills, I was still troubled over just how to serve both God and the church as a whole when I'm in prison and so many miles separated from you. Well, perhaps God will take this letter as a small offering, an indication that I am willing to help in any way I can. . . .

I recently received the directory of Cherry Hills members, the church directory. As I leafed through the pages, God spoke to me. Not like in some Cecil B. De Mille movie but in the quiet voice that has become familiar to me. "Even though you're in prison, you can still pray." So I started with the A's in the church directory, and I've begun to pray for each of you. What a joy it has been for me. I firmly believe that God answers prayer so I've prayed that you'll come to understand, as I have, that the question is not, to be or not to be, but rather who's to be. Once that's decided, to be is enough for any person. May God bless you all so you may, in turn, be a blessing to others for the glory of His name.

Here is a just man. He's not just in the eyes of the State of Mississippi, for in their eyes he's an ex-drug addict and convicted murderer serving a life sentence in a federal prison. But he is just in the sight of God, and he is just before the laws of God. He is just only because he acknowledged his sin and, in repentance, came to Jesus Christ asking for mercy, grace, and forgiveness. He invited Christ to be the Lord of his life and his Savior from sin, and the Holy Spirit bears witness by his transformed life.

God is greatly using him. He led twenty-six people to Jesus Christ during one year in prison. Likewise, God greatly wants to use you where you are. But that can only happen when you decide that you want to become just. You can become just only by placing your faith in Jesus Christ, the Just One, who promises to impute His righteousness to you and forgive your sins.

When you embrace Christ as your Lord and Savior, you become a child of God. You seek to live a righteous life that is found only in Jesus Christ, the Just and Righteous One. But that's only part of what it means to become just.

A Just Person Seeks Justice

Obviously, we don't live in a just world. Wicked people are not always punished. Righteous people are not always rewarded. People are not always treated fairly. But if you are a Christian — a person whom God has declared righteous through faith in Jesus Christ and who has made a commitment to live each day with the desire to do His will on earth — you are to seek to make this world a better place.

About 2,500 years ago, as told in the biblical book of Daniel, a man named Belshazzar ruled the Babylonian Empire. He was not a just ruler. He did not treat people equally. He did not punish the wicked. He did not reward the righteous. Throughout his reign he acted in utterly depraved ways and practiced every kind of fornication.

One day King Belshazzar threw a huge party in his banquet hall. A thousand of his nobles were present, as were all of his wives, concubines, and friends. Inebriated and flushed with his importance, the king ordered his servants to bring in the gold and silver goblets that his father Nebuchadnezzar had confiscated from the Israelites' temple in Jerusalem years earlier. Then the riotous people filled the sacred goblets with wine, became more drunk, and

> praised the gods of gold and silver, of bronze, iron, wood and stone. Suddenly the fingers of a human hand appeared and wrote on the plaster of the wall, near the lampstand in the royal palace. The king

watched the hand as it wrote. His face turned pale
and he was so frightened that his knees knocked
together and his legs gave way.

Daniel 5:4-6

In desperation the king summoned his enchanters, astrologers,
and diviners; but they could not read the words that the hand had
written. Then the queen reminded the king of Daniel, and Daniel was
summoned.

"If you can read this writing and tell me what it means," the king
promised, "you will be exalted as the third highest ruler in the kingdom."

Although he didn't want the riches and the honor, Daniel spoke
the words of God to King Belshazzar. He spoke of the arrogance of the
king's father and of how God had made his father mentally ill until he
acknowledged God's sovereignty. He also spoke of Belshazzar's pride,
idol worship, and refusal to honor God. Then Daniel explained the words
God had written:

> MENE, MENE, TEKEL, PARSIN.
> *Mene*: God has numbered the days of your reign and
> brought it to an end.
> *Tekel*: You have been weighed on the scales and found
> wanting.
> *Peres*: Your kingdom is divided and given to the
> Medes and Persians.

Daniel 5:26-28

That very night justice was served. The armies of the Medo-
Persian Empire poured into the royal city of Babylon, and King
Belshazzar was killed. The Babylonian kingdom was then divided.

This kind of event hasn't happened often — in the biblical record
or in history as a whole. God doesn't normally establish justice during
this age of the world. He doesn't normally intervene in human history

in this way. He doesn't normally cause wicked people to die prematurely. Many malignant rulers reign for a long time, and many benign rulers die young. Many criminals live in lavish estates and die of old age. We simply don't live in a just world.

The Bible tells us that justice waits for God's timing. In this world justice is seldom served, but at the judgment seat complete justice will be served when God judges all people through Christ Jesus. One day He will establish justice in heaven and on earth; but until that day comes, He has entrusted justice to you and to me. God has commissioned us as Christians to make this world a more just place — to bring justice into our world.

Years ago I read a magazine article about a Texan named Donald Dixon. He purchased a small savings and loan in Texas in 1982 and built it into one of the largest savings and loan in that state. But the United States Department of Justice, upon investigating him, alleged that Dixon used some of the savings and loan's money to buy a California beach home, to travel around the world, to throw lavish parties, to hire prostitutes, to make illegal contributions to politicians and political candidates, and to buy airplanes. After examining his records for three years, the United States Department of Justice brought a thirty-eight count criminal indictment against him.

In contrast, perhaps thousands of other people have committed crimes similar to Donald Dixon's crime, but many of them may never be punished. Why? It costs billions of dollars for the United States Department of Justice to investigate and to prosecute criminals. Moreover, our judicial system doesn't have the staff needed to handle the careful research required to prepare and to prosecute all of the cases.

We live in a fallen world. Even if governments are committed to establishing justice, it's not easy for them to do it. There are far more criminals in this world than prison cells. There are far more criminals in this world than police officers. But this seemingly insurmountable problem is not simply the problem of governments.

As Christians it is *our* problem. It's easy for those of us who are evangelical Christians to focus only on proclaiming the Gospel of salvation. Yes, that is to be our primary goal because Christ died to save sinners. But we are not to ignore social justice! God commands us to

Seek justice, encourage the oppressed. Defend the cause of the fatherless, plead the case of the widow.

Isaiah 1:17

When we do so, God promises to reward us:

If you do away with the yoke of oppression, . . . and if you spend yourselves in behalf of the hungry and satisfy the needs of the oppressed, then your light will rise in the darkness, and your night will become like the noonday. The Lord will guide you always; he will satisfy your needs in a sun-scorched land and will strengthen your frame.

Isaiah 58:9-11

Jesus Christ loves every person, for we are all created in the image of God. But there is much injustice in our world. As Christians we must not remain silent. We must speak out. That's why we are called to vote. That's why we are called to participate in jury duty. That's why we are called to bring God's truth into our speaking and writing. That's why we are called to pray.

God calls us to do anything and everything we can within the law to fight injustice in our world. As representatives of Jesus Christ, we must take action to implement justice even when such actions are not easy and may bear tough consequences.

In 1860, only 139 years ago, slavery was legal in America. The law was used to oppress about four million slaves who toiled in the southern slave states. The slaves were not allowed to own property. They were not allowed to bear witness. They were not allowed to marry.

Chapter Eleven: Justice

When these slaves sought to learn how to read and to write in order to better themselves, the United States government passed a law in 1831 that made it illegal to teach a slave to read or write. When white men had sexual relations with their slave women, the resulting children claimed to be free because their fathers were free. The United States government passed a law stating that children were only born free if their mothers were free. Thus white men were free to have sexual relations with their slaves and not worry about how they treated the resulting offspring.

Did millions of Americans during that time know that slavery was wrong? Yes. Did many Christians know that slavery was wrong? Yes. Most, however, remained silent. They didn't obey God. They didn't seek justice.

The list of injustices goes on and on. In the early 1800's women in the United States began their crusade for women's suffrage. Yet it was not until 1920 that the required number of states ratified what became known as the 19th Amendment. Did many Christian men know that prohibiting women from voting was wrong? Sure, but most men said nothing. Each year in this country more than a million babies are aborted. In fact, since the 1973 *Roe v. Wade* decision legalized abortion, more than thirty-five million babies have been aborted. How can we be silent about this national nightmare?

God has called Christians to make this world a better place — to apply His truths to culture, to obey Him, and to be salt and light in a world of spiritual darkness so that His will might be done on earth as it is in heaven.

> And what does the Lord require of you? To act justly and to love mercy and to walk humbly with your God.
>
> Micah 6:8

Wisdom

CHAPTER TWELVE

As a human baby grows, baby teeth begin to appear. Most children have them by age two. There are twenty of these temporary, deciduous teeth; and they are gradually pushed out and replaced by thirty-two permanent teeth, which began to grow even before birth. The first permanent teeth to arrive are the central incisors. The last permanent teeth to arrive are the third molars. They are often called wisdom teeth because they do not normally appear until a person is at least seventeen years old. The thought behind the term "wisdom teeth" is that the person who has them should have some measure of wisdom. Unfortunately, we all know that wisdom doesn't necessarily come with age. Some people never obtain much wisdom—no matter how long they live! According to the Bible, true wisdom is rare.

True Wisdom Comes Only From God

You are probably familar with Richard Burton, the actor; but you may not be familiar with Sir Richard Burton, a brilliant nineteenth-century explorer and author. Known for his English translation of *The Book of the Thousand Nights,* he became most famous for the adventure that he and his friend John Speke had in central Africa in 1858. Seeking the source of the Nile, he became the first European in modern times to view Lake Tanganyika. (Burton and Speke's explorations were made into a movie titled *Mountains of the Moon,* released in 1990.)

But Sir Richard Burton faced a much greater quest in his lifetime than finding the source of the Nile. He sought the source of true wisdom, and he risked his life to find it. In 1853, he disguised himself as an Afghan doctor and made his way to Mecca and to Medina to the jealously guarded shrines of Islam. There he entered places where no Islamic unbeliever is allowed to go. In 1860, Burton came to America and traveled by covered wagon to Utah. There he began to fellowship with the Mormons. He stayed for years. Why? He still sought the source of true wisdom. In 1888, Burton was knighted, but he died in spiritual darkness in 1890. Although he knew that God was the source of wisdom, he never found God in his study of Islam or Mormonism.

Do you, like Sir Richard, want to find true wisdom? It can only come from God.

James, the brother of Jesus wrote,

> If any of you lacks wisdom, he should ask God, . . .
> and it will be given to him.
>
> James 1:5

The apostle Paul wrote,

> we preach Christ crucified, a stumbling block to Jews and foolishness to Gentiles, but to those whom God has called, both Jews and Greeks, Christ the power of God and *the wisdom of God.*
>
> 1 Corinthians 1:23-24, italics added

Truly, Jesus is the source of true wisdom.

Maybe you are brilliant. Maybe you have an IQ above two hundred. Maybe you received a perfect SAT score. Maybe you graduated with honors from the Massachusetts Institute of Technology. Maybe you've read hundreds or even thousands of books. Yet none of these will give you wisdom or demonstrate that you have gained it. According to the Bible, many brilliant people are, in fact, fools.

You see, true wisdom is not the same as knowledge. True wisdom is not the same as intelligence. True wisdom is not the same as common sense. While each of these can be obtained through personal effort and discipline, true wisdom is a gift; and it comes only from God through Jesus Christ.

You probably own a color television set. But if you are interested in watching a certain movie or a live boxing match, just because you own a television set doesn't mean you'll be able to watch either of these programs. You will need to install special equipment and subscribe to the cable channels that carry these particular programs. If you don't have the equipment installed and pay the extra money, your television set won't receive what the cable channels are broadcasting.

Likewise, God wants us to understand that most people today are not subscribing to what might be termed the "wisdom channel." Most people have ears to hear, but they cannot hear Jesus' wisdom. They have eyes to see, but they cannot see His wisdom. The only way they will be capable of receiving and hearing the wisdom of God is by meeting Jesus Christ through faith and subscribing to His truths. Only then does God send His Holy Spirit to live within them so that they can receive His wisdom.

The Goal and Purpose of True Wisdom

When we understand the goal and the purpose of true wisdom, we will better understand the wisdom of God. Is the goal and the purpose of true wisdom to obtain a fulfilled life? Amass earthly riches? Share wise counsel with people? Evaluate current trends and predict future ones? No. The goal and the purpose of true wisdom is to seek Jesus Christ's kingdom and character. Everything else is foolishness.

The wisdom of this world dictates that people seek to build their own kingdoms. The wisdom of this world dictates that people should satisfy themselves. The wisdom of this world dictates that people should meet their own needs. *After all,* many people think, *if I don't meet my needs, no one else will meet them.* In contrast, Jesus told His followers,

> Do not worry, saying, 'What shall we eat?' or 'What shall we drink?' or 'What shall we wear?' For the pagans run after all these things, and your heavenly Father knows that you need them. But seek first his kingdom and his righteousness, and all these things will be given to you as well.
>
> Matthew 6:31-33

Truly, the wisdom of God is antithetical to the wisdom of the world.

As I worked on this book, the movie *Titanic* was a box office hit. During its maiden voyage from Southampton, England, to New York City, the Titanic sank in the North Atlantic Ocean on April 14, 1912, drowning 1,517 people. Most of the people who survived the tragic sinking were women and children. Some have shared their stories.

One wealthy woman, who was seated in a lifeboat that was ready to leave the sinking ship, suddenly exclaimed, "I have to go back to my stateroom. It's urgent."

A nearby person responded, "If you don't come back in three minutes, we're going to give your place to somebody else."

The woman ran desperately across the tilting deck. She entered the gambling hall where money was ankle deep in some places, but she didn't reach down. She yanked open the door to her stateroom and fumbled amidst her diamond rings, golden bracelets, and golden necklaces. Searching, she found the objects of her desire, three oranges. Frantically, she ran back to the lifeboat.

Amazing. Thirty minutes earlier, she wouldn't have accepted a crate of oranges in exchange for her smallest diamond. Now a crate of diamonds wasn't worth three oranges. She had gained an entirely new perspective on life. She had realized that the three oranges might mean the difference between life and death for her and the other people in the boat.

If you are a Christian, this has happened to you. Your reality is quite different from that of the secular world. Other people might say that your perspective toward life is upside down. Other people might even consider you a fool for living according to the eternal perspective God has given you. But if you have the wisdom of Christ, you know that the ways of this world are like a sinking ship. The many pleasures, possessions, and titles that the world seeks will never lead to genuine fulfillment and joy. From an eternal perspective all that matters is pursuing the kingdom of Christ and His righteousness. Everything else is vanity. Solomon, the wisest person who ever lived, said this numerous times in Ecclesiastes.

Do you remember Jesus' story of the rich man (Luke 12:16-21)? A rich man owned fertile land, which produced a bumper crop. He thought, *What am I going to do? I have no place in which to store all of these crops. I'll tear down my barns and build bigger ones in which I can store all my grain and my goods.* As Jesus continued the story, the rich man said to himself, "You have plenty of good things laid up for many years. Take life easy; eat, drink and be merry."

In response, God said to him, "You fool! This very night your life will be demanded from you. Then who will get what you have prepared for yourself?"

In what ways did this rich man think and act foolishly? He followed the wisdom of the world. He did everything that the world today tells us to do. He sought security through the accumulation of wealth. He sought happiness and fulfillment by adopting a life of ease. But in the sight of God, these pursuits are mere foolishness.

Jesus Christ is the only genuine source of security. Knowing the character of Christ and serving Him and His kingdom provide the only genuine source of joy. Therein lies the wisdom of God.

One weekend Barbara and I traveled to Washington, D.C. where we joined a group of Christians for a conference. Stuart Briscoe, one of the conference speakers, made this comment: "The world seeks three things—comfort, profit, and popularity." After evaluating his words, I realize how true this is, even of me. I know that some of the world's thinking is anchored in my mind. I am tempted to seek comfort, profit, and popularity. I am drawn to seek what the world believes is important and what the world promises will fulfill me.

I still remember what Stuart said next. "If you have the wisdom of God, you do not seek these things. You don't seek comfort, profit, or popularity. If you have the wisdom of God, then you seek first the kingdom of God and the character of Christ. You seek what is good and what is true and what is right." Maybe he recalled John's words that the person who "does what is right is righteous" (1 John 3:7). Perhaps he was thinking of Paul's challenging words in Philippians 4:8.

> Whatever is true, whatever is noble, whatever is right, whatever is pure, whatever is lovely, whatever is admirable—if anything is excellent or praiseworthy—think about such things.

In our culture what is right in God's eyes is not always profitable. Those involved in business, know this is true. What is right in God's eyes is not necessarily popular or comfortable. Mother Teresa experienced many uncomfortable moments while tending dying people in India.

The question is, "What are *we* pursuing in life?" What do we seek? Is it comfort? Is it profit? Is it popularity? Or are we prayerfully trying to put Jesus Christ and His kingdom first in all that we do? If we seek anything else but the kingdom of God and His righteousness, we'll never find satisfaction. But if we seek God, He will provide everything we need.

In the United States we celebrate Mother's Day and Father's Day. The goal is to honor mothers and fathers. Most of us also celebrate the birthdays of family members and friends and honor these people in special ways with presents, cake and ice cream, and parties.

Chapter Twelve: Wisdom

But who does God want to honor? Who are the people that are wise and pleasing in His sight? I can promise you, on the authority of God's Word, that God is pleased with every man, woman, boy, and girl who seeks first the kingdom of Christ and His righteousness. Such a person is wise indeed. It is the fool who primarily pursues profit, comfort, and popularity.

If we seek first Christ's kingdom and His righteousness, our perspective toward money, our family, our job, and even our physical health will be completely different from the perspective held by the world. We'll view money as a tool we can primarily use to support the service of Christ. We'll want to honor God in the way we meet the needs of our family and do our job. We'll no longer exercise for the sake of vanity. Rather we'll exercise because we want to be a good steward of what God has given us — to be healthy for the sake of serving the kingdom of God and to keep our ministry from being cut short unnecessarily.

Perhaps you have heard of Cleopatra's Needles. These two giant obelisks were built more than three thousand years ago in Egypt during the reign of Pharaoh Thutmose III, who ruled Egypt during the 1400's B.C. Ramses II also inscribed the obelisks about two hundred years later, and about 10 B.C. they were moved from the sun temple at Heliopolis to Alexandria and raised toward the heavens in order to decorate a palace.

Today these ancient obelisks still stand tall. One of them, a gift from Egypt to the British, stands in London, England, along the Thames River. The other, given to the United States by Egypt, is sixty-nine feet tall, weighs more than two hundred tons, and was erected in New York City's Central Park in 1881.

According to Pliny the Elder, an historian who died in Pompeii during the eruption of Mount Vesuvius, when Cleopatra's Needles were ready to be raised upright in Alexandria, the Pharaoh didn't want the supervising engineer to make a mistake. He didn't want the obelisks to fall or to be broken. Therefore, the Pharaoh took the engineer's two sons and had one bound to each obelisk. The lives of the engineer's sons were thus tied to his performance. If the engineer made a mistake, one or both of his sons would die.

Likewise, for those of us who are parents, the lives of our children are tied to our performances. If we seek earthly comfort, profit, and popularity, our children will suffer negative consequences. But if we seek first the kingdom of Christ and His righteousness, our families will experience the blessings of God.

Which of us is wise and understanding? Let us seek first Christ's kingdom, and He will provide us with everything we need.

Self-Control

CHAPTER THIRTEEN

In 1864, a drunken man tripped and severely gashed his head on a bedside table. Blood flowed freely as he lay sprawled on the floor until a chambermaid entered the room. Transported from the rundown American Hotel in New York City to Belleview Hospital, the unconscious man died despite doctors' frantic efforts.

"It's no big loss," some people muttered. "He is probably just a nameless bum who has never done anything with his life and never would have done anything."

Local authorities, however, soon discovered that the man's name was Stephen Collins Foster, one of the most beloved song writers in nineteenth-century America. He had written "My Old Kentucky Home," which became the state song for Kentucky and is still sung before the Kentucky Derby and other official occasions. He had written "Oh! Susanna," a favorite song of the 49ers during the California gold rush. He had written "Camp Town Races," "Jeanie With The Light Brown Hair," "Beautiful Dreamer," and hundreds of other beloved songs.

Yet there he lay, dead at age thirty-eight, a tragic victim of alcohol. In his pocket he had less than forty cents and a scrap of paper on which he had scribbled, "dear friends and gentle hearts." Perhaps that was the beginning of another song, but he never finished it. Alcohol cut short his creative talent.

Today medical doctors and scientists have a better understanding of alcoholism. They tell us that alcoholics probably have a deficiency of endorphins, morphine-like compounds produced naturally by the body, in their brains. Endorphins help relieve pain, control stress, and promote a sense of well being. While many medical doctors believe that alcoholics use alcohol to compensate for a lack of endorphins, tragically the consumption of alcohol actually decreases the number of endorphines produced. As a result the alcoholic ends up drinking even more, and the downward spiral continues.

Scientists tell us that a percentage of the world's population has a chemical predisposition toward alcoholism. That may explain why millions of people in the United States and around the world are alcoholics. Today many people would say that Stephen Collins Foster was a tragic victim of the disease called alcoholism. But years ago people viewed alcoholics much differently. In 1864, Stephen Collins Foster was not an alcoholic, a victim of a disease; he was simply a drunk who lacked self-control.

Certainly, the modern view of alcoholism is much more scientific. Certainly, this modern view that alcoholics are victims of their addiction also provides a framework for demonstrating more compassion and love toward alcoholics. Certainly, any addiction, including alcoholism, is strong. Certainly, any addiction has a psychological dimension to it. Certainly, addicted people deserve to be loved and to receive compassion. But they are not simply helpless victims of their addictions as many people in this generation want to believe.

The modern view of addiction may be a more superior view, but it's not an adequate view. Why? Biblically speaking, we are not simply victims of our addictions. According to the Bible, God has given us some measure of free will. We have volition. We are morally culpable. God tells us that one day we will each give an account of all our thoughts and actions. He calls us to assume some measure of responsibility.

Today people who are sexually promiscuous may be considered

victims of sexual addiction. People who overeat may be considered victims of eating disorders. People who abuse drugs may be considered victims of drug addiction. Even people who break serious laws may receive lenient sentences if they are considered victims of a bad home life, peer pressure, or a chemical imbalance. They were, therefore, unable to exercise complete control over their actions.

Yes, many factors influence our thoughts and behaviors and cause us to respond in certain ways. But God still wants each of us to accept responsibility for our actions. In other words, He wants us to exercise some measure of self-control. Yet why do so many people in the world today, Christians included, lack self-control?

We Do Not Avail Ourselves of the Power of Christ

Within recent years scientists have used giant radio telescopes to discover an extraordinary power, a black hole, at the center of our Milky Way Galaxy. Although our line of sight to it is blocked by space and star matter, this power is about twenty-five thousand light years away and is reportedly consuming stars, planets, and entire solar systems.

At the center of each of our lives, there is also what could be termed a black hole. It is called sin, and it wants to take us into oblivion. Sometimes we don't feel the tug of sin much. Other times we can barely resist its pull. We don't seem to have the power, strength, or self-control to resist it; and we're sucked into its vortex. As the apostle Paul wrote, "I do not understand what I do. For what I want to do I do not do, but what I hate I do" (Romans 7:15).

Yet if we have believed in Jesus Christ as Lord and Savior, divine power has entered our lives that is much greater than the black hole of sin. The Bible says that the Holy Spirit Himself resides in us (Romans 8:11) and that He has awesome, unbelievable, incomprehensible power.

On May 18, 1980, more than one thousand feet of the top of Mount St. Helens exploded into the air, devastating part of the Cascade Mountains in the state of Washington. Incredibly, 150-foot Douglas Fir trees seventeen miles from the epicenter of the volcanic eruption were knocked down. In fact, the eruption destroyed 3.2 billion board feet of lumber, enough lumber to build two hundred thousand three-bedroom homes. Researchers say that the force of the blast was equivalent to ten million tons of exploding TNT! Although most of the people in the region had been evacuated, sixty people died. Most of them were killed by three-hundred-degree temperatures radiating from the core of the blast at two hundred miles per hour. One of the greatest demonstrations of nature's power witnessed in recent times, the Mount St. Helens' eruption, nevertheless, pales in comparison to the power of the Son of God.

Two words used in the Bible are translated "power." The Greek word *exousia* refers to political, governmental power, such as the power that kings wield. The other Greek word *dunamis* refers to raw, physical power. This is the type of power demonstrated during the eruption of Mount St. Helens. This word is the source of the word *dynamite*.

Both *exousia* and *dunamis* are used in the Bible to describe the person of Jesus Christ. First, He possesses governmental power because He is the King of kings and the Lord of lords. One day all the nations of this world will submit to Him. Second, He possesses raw, physical power. After all, He created the earth. The heavens are the work of His hands, and He sustains the universe by His word of power. (See John 1:1-3, Colossians 1:16-17, and Hebrews 1:1-2.)

The Greek word *enkrates,* translated "self-control," is derived from the Greek word *kratos* that means "strength" and the word *en* that means "within" or "inner." Thus self-control, biblically speaking, is an inner strength or a strength from within.

For those of us who are Christians, God's incomprehensible power lies within us. God's power working through us gives self-control. In order to really obtain self-control — to see the power of God released through us — we must avail ourselves of His power and His strength that is within us. That's why self-control is listed in Galatians 5:22-23 as a fruit of the Holy Spirit: "love, joy, peace, patience, kindness, goodness, faithfulness, gentleness, and *self-control.*" Any other source of self-control is rooted in the flesh, in our own sinful strength.

As Christians, every time we read the Bible God's power is released within us. David understood this and wrote, "I have hidden your word in my heart that I might not sin against you" (Psalm 119:11). Every time we get down on our knees and pray, in some measure His power is released within us. Every time we fellowship with other Christians, in some measure His power is released within us to enable us to obtain greater self-control. Every time we confess our sins to a few other believers and ask them to pray over us and lay hands on us in prayer, in some measure His power is released within us.

God understands our need for self-control, and He makes His power available to us. But we have to ask for it. The apostle James wrote, "You do not have, because you do not ask God" (James 4:2). Jesus Himself said,

> Which of you, if his son asks for bread, will give him a stone? Or if he asks for a fish, will give him a snake? If you, then, though you are evil, know how to give good gifts to your children, how much more will your Father in heaven give good gifts to those who ask him!
>
> Matthew 7:9-11

We Are Not Willing to Pay the Price

Many of us lack self-control because we do not avail ourselves of the power of Jesus Christ within us. Equally, many of us lack self-control because we are not willing to pay the price to become more like Jesus.

Sanctification brings a certain amount of suffering into our lives. A certain amount of pain comes into our lives when we pursue Christlikeness. We can't possibly exercise self-control in our lives without enduring some discomfort or paying some price.

Vice & Virtue: The Battle Within

Each fourth of July many of us in the United States celebrate our nation's independence. We get together with family members and/or friends. We have barbecues. We watch three-thousand-horsepower cars race on speedways. We visit national parks. We watch fireworks fill the sky.

But on July 4, 1776, when the Second Continental Congress officially adopted the final draft of the Declaration of Independence that had been approved by vote on July 2, the men who signed it knew that they would pay a price. As they signed this document, these fifty-six men pledged their lives, fortunes, and sacred honor that this nation might be born and its people might obtain independence. No one understood this more clearly than Thomas Jefferson, who had written it, and John Adams and Benjamin Franklin, who had made minor alterations.

The resulting War of Independence, which actually began at the Battle of Bunker Hill on June 17, 1775, continued for nearly seven years after the signing of the Declaration of Independence in 1776. History chronicles what took place at Lexington, Concord, Bunker Hill, Yorktown, and Trenton. Victories were won. Defeats were suffered. Battle sites were littered with the dead and the dying.

Heroes were forged during those years. Each of the fifty-six men who signed the Declaration of Independence paid a high price for our freedom. Many lost their homes, and many lost their lives. The men who would become the first five Presidents of the United States—George Washington, John Adams, Thomas Jefferson, James Madison, and James Monroe—made personal sacrifices in order to help gain our nation's independence. For example, James Madison fought in the Battle of Trenton where he suffered a gun shot wound to his shoulder. George Washington crossed the Delaware River at Trenton at Christmastime in hopes of winning the Battle of Trenton. He and ten thousand troops withstood the unbearable weather conditions at Valley Forge, Pennsylvania, during the winters of 1777 and 1778.

Our seventh President, Andrew Jackson was only thirteen years

Chapter Thirteen: Self-Control

old at the time but was present at the Battle of Hanging Rock in August of 1780. The following April, at the age of fourteen, he was captured by the British while he was at the home of his cousin. A British soldier sliced Jackson's head and left hand with a sword because the young man refused to polish the boots of the British officer in charge. He was then forced to undergo a forty-mile march without food, water, or medical care before spending time in a British prisoner-of-war camp.

As Christians we are citizens of the kingdom of heaven. This world is truly not our home. Our real destiny is heaven where we will live for untold billions of years. We will spend only a brief time here on earth, and it will be a time of suffering. It will also be a time of spiritual battle. The kingdom of God is at war with evil and the forces of darkness. As Christians we seek independence from sin, which we can combat with many spiritual weapons. (See Ephesians 6:10-18.) Self-control is also in our arsenal of weapons; but if we are going to join in the spiritual battle, we must willingly pay the price. In 2 Peter 1:3-7, we read,

> His [God's] divine power has given us everything we need for life and godliness through our knowledge of him who called us by his own glory and goodness. Through these he has given us his very great and precious promises, so that through them you may participate in the divine nature and escape the corruption in the world caused by evil desires. For this very reason, *make every effort* to add to your faith goodness; and to goodness, knowledge; and to knowledge, *self-control*; and to self-control, perseverance; and to perseverance, godliness; and to godliness, brotherly kindness; and to brotherly kindness, love (italics added).

The Greek word *krateo*, translated "make every effort," means "to struggle" and "to strive." Are you willing to struggle and to strive to achieve self-control? It's not easy to do today. You'll face temptations everyday. But think of the consequences if you don't! A person without self-control is defenseless. Solomon wrote, "Like a city whose walls are broken down is a man who lacks self-control" (Proverbs 25:28).

Pay attention to the call of God today. Realize that His power lies within you. Be willing to pay the price to obtain self-control, the fruit of the Holy Spirit.

Courage

CHAPTER FOURTEEN

In 1951, fear entered the lives of people working at a nuclear reactor site near Chalk River, Canada. The reactor's core was leaking radiation badly and had to be fixed. But there would be no margin for error. The consequences of a full meltdown would be horrible.

A twenty-six-year-old lieutenant in the United States Navy was flown in to provide assistance. He understood nuclear-reactor technology and nuclear physics. He had served with the Atomic Energy Commission. He had high-security clearance status; and he understood the risks of disassembling the reactor core, a process that had to be completed piece by piece.

He was told that even though he wore a special radiation suit his body would be bombarded in a few seconds by the maximum allowable amount of radiation a human being could safely endure in a year's time. He was told that he might become sterile, that he might develop cancer, and that he might even die in that mouth of manmade hell. But somebody had to fix the reactor.

Having practiced disassembling a replica of the reactor core, the day came for him to disassemble the device. He took the risk and successfully disassembled it, thereby, averting the meltdown.

Fortunately, this knowledgeable and courageous man didn't become sterile, develop cancer, or die next to the reactor core. In fact, he later became the governor of Georgia and the President of the United States! His name is Jimmy Carter.

Our nation, along with many other nations, exalts courage. In the United States we give the Congressional Medal of Honor, the Silver Star, and the Bronze Star to courageous people. Britain gives the Victoria Cross. Germany gives the Iron Cross. But did you know that, according to Scripture, God also exalts courage? In fact, that's why early Christians identified courage as one of the seven cardinal virtues. Courage is precious to God for two reasons.

God Uses Courageous Christians to Transform the World

If you are a Christian and have courage, Christ can use you to transform the world! Do you believe that?

Perhaps you've seen photographs of the Roman Colosseum in which gladiators, men trained by the Roman Empire, fought to the death every afternoon in order to entertain the Roman masses and to try to satisfy their thirst for blood. Each light-armored gladiator was given a sword, a shield, a trident, and a helmet; and from 264 B.C. until 404 A.D., gladiatorial combat was featured in Roman life. During four months in 107 A.D., Emperor Trajan sent ten thousand gladiators into the arena.

Yet many people tried to stop it. In 73 B.C., for example, a gladiator named Spartacus joined with other gladiators and about seventy thousand slaves in a revolt against Roman authority. Spartacus was killed in 71 B.C., and the combat continued.

In 404 A.D., a Syrian monk named Telemikous entered the arena floor of the Colosseum one afternoon. The animals had already fought in the morning, and now the gladiators fought among themselves. In the midst of the clanging swords, the cries, and the blood, Telemikous cried out to the audience. His voice rang loudly: "No more! No more blood! No more inhumanity to man! No more death! Human life is precious! God grieves in heaven!"

Chapter Fourteen: Courage

The people in the stands became enraged at this courageous Christian. They mocked him and threw objects at him. Caught up in the excitement, the gladiators attacked him; and a sword pierced him. The gentle monk fell to the ground and died.

Suddenly, the entire Colosseum fell silent. For the first time the people whose bloodthirst had been beyond satiation recognized the horror of what they had once called entertainment. For the first time Emperor Honorius recognized that an event so horrible had to be halted. Because of Telemikous' courage and his ensuing death, Honorius abolished gladiatorial combat that day throughout the Roman Empire.

Jesus Christ used one Christian's courage to transform a part of the world that day; and He wants to use you, too, if you will choose to be courageous. Will you take the Gospel into your world? Into your neighborhood? Into your workplace? Into your home? Nothing will transform the world like the Gospel message and the power of God that underlies it. It's the only power that can possibly transform the human heart.

At a Fellowship of Christian Athletes gathering that I attended in Washington, D.C., former Vice President Dan Quayle emphasized that our nation needs, above all else, Christian men and women who are willing to stand up courageously for biblical truth.

Today our nation needs Christians who will speak out and who will take a stand against issues, such as the growing apostasy in mainline Protestant denominations; abortion, which kills more than a million babies every year and has killed more than thirty-five million babies since the *Roe v. Wade* decision in 1973; the multibillion-dollar pornography business, which sexually exploits children and is allegedly protected by the United States Constitution; and the growing anti-Christian biases demonstrated by the media and entertainment industries.

It has always required courage to stand for biblical truth, and Christ wants to use you. One Christian can make a great difference. Perhaps you remember hearing about Bridget Murgens, a Christian student who attended West Side High School in Omaha, Nebraska. She and other high school Christian friends decided that they wanted to meet voluntarily after school for a time of Bible study and prayer. *After all,* they reasoned, *other groups of students are meeting in classrooms on a voluntary basis.* The girls asked the school administration for permission; their request was denied. The reason? Administrators said that such a meeting would violate the separation of church and state.

But Bridget didn't simply acquiesce. She stood firm. Courageously, she determined to fight the administration's ruling. Finally, her case worked its way to the United States Supreme Court; and because of one student's courage, a landmark legal decision was made. In an 8 to 1 decision, the Supreme Court Justices sided with Bridget stating:

> In all public schools across this nation, if Christians want to assemble freely, they should have that right if the school is also allowing other groups to assemble freely.

As I reflect on the early church and, particularly, on the first-century Christians who took the Gospel to the far corners of their known world, I marvel at their courage. According to church tradition, Matthew was killed by a sword in Ethiopia while serving as a missionary for Jesus Christ. Mark was killed in Alexandria, Egypt, where he was dragged through the streets of the city because of his testimony to Jesus Christ. Luke, the beloved physician who loved Jesus more than his earthly life, was hanged from an olive tree in Greece. Emperor Nero, who also beheaded the apostle Paul at Three Fountains in Rome, crucified Peter upside down in Rome. Philip was strung from a pillar and strangled in the city of Heropolis in the Province of Peregia in Asia Minor (modern-day Turkey). James the Greater was beheaded in Jerusalem. James the Less was beaten to death by a club. James, the brother of Jesus and head of the Jerusalem church, was pushed off the pinnacle of a temple as he proclaimed the Gospel of Christ. He survived the fall but was stoned to death where he landed.

The list continues. Jude, the brother of Jesus, was shot with arrows because of his testimony. Andrew, Simon Peter's brother, was crucified but preached the love, grace, and mercy of Jesus to his tormentors until he drew his last breath. Bartholomew was beaten to death. Barnabas, whom the New Testament writers called an apostle, was stoned to death by an angry Jewish mob in the city of Selonica because he said that Jesus was the Messiah. Matthias, who was chosen to replace Judas Iscariot, was stoned to death and then beheaded. Thomas was run through with a lance in the distant land of Coromendel where he served as a missionary. According to church tradition, only the apostle John didn't die a martyr. Yet he suffered a great deal while imprisoned by Emperor Domitian on the island of Patmos.

Truly, the foundation of the early church was built on the blood of courageous men and women who in the power of God transformed the world. They turned the world upside down. Eventually, Christianity conquered the entire Roman Empire because men and women were courageous for Jesus Christ.

Unfortunately, in our culture today many Christians basically live to obtain health and wealth. Prosperity teaching has found fertile soil in the United States and in other countries. The question, "What's in it for me?" has become quite popular. In contrast, Jesus Christ said,

> If anyone would come after me, he must deny himself and take up his cross and follow me. For whoever wants to save his life will lose it, but whoever loses his life for me will find it.
>
> Matthew 16:24-25

God Uses Courage to Keep the World from Transforming Christians

If you are a Christian who is living courageously, Christ can use you to transform the world; and He can keep the world from transforming you. Do you remember what Paul wrote in Romans 12:2? "Do not conform any longer to the pattern of this world, but be transformed by the renewing of your mind." You and I must not allow the world to squeeze us into its mold. It takes courage to say *no* and to resist the world's transforming power.

In 1924, Eric Liddell was to run the one-hundred-meter race during the Olympic Games in Paris. He had trained for years to run that race, honing his body to reach its peak of endurance and speed. But when he arrived in Paris and learned that the race would be run on Sunday, he courageously withdrew from the race. Seeking to honor the Lord's day, he refused to run on Sunday despite the intense pressure from many people who told him to set aside his convictions in order to run. People all over the world called him a fool. "Why give up so much," they questioned, "for so little?"

Then a runner withdrew from the four-hundred-meter race. This allowed Liddell to participate in the games by running on a different day of the week. Liddell wasn't expected to place, much less to win. Yet, he did win. In fact, not only did he receive the Olympic gold, but he also established a new Olympic record with a time of 47.6 seconds!

Liddell later became a missionary for Jesus Christ in China. Faithful and courageous to the end, he died in a prisoner-of-war camp in 1945. The movie *Chariots of Fire* tells part of his story.

Maybe you don't agree with the stand that Eric Liddell took regarding athletic competition on Sunday, but I'm sure you'll agree with me that he had courage. He was willing to say *no*, no matter what the cost. He sought to be molded by Christ and not by the world. He illustrates the kind of Christians Jesus Christ is looking for: Christians who will say *no* to the world for the sake of Christ and His kingdom and who desire only to be molded by Jesus Christ.

Chapter Fourteen: Courage

In the Texas city of San Antonio stands the Alamo. Originally built to be a church and monastery, the Alamo became famous during the Texans' battle for independence from Mexico in 1836. General Antonio Lopez de Santa Anna and more than five thousand Mexican soldiers besieged and attacked Colonel William Travis and 182 defenders who had chosen to make a final stand for Texas' separation and independence.

Many heroes, including David Crockett the frontiersman and Jim Bowie the legendary adventurer, stood on the walls of the Alamo when the battle began. But perhaps the greatest hero was James Bonham whom Colonel Travis sent out while the Alamo was under siege. Sneaking out one night, Bonham threaded his way through the Mexican soldiers and hiked ninety miles to the town of Goliad. There he petitioned the army garrison, pleading for troops to come to the Alamo's rescue. But no help could be spared.

What did Bonham do then? Did he go to another part of Texas and settle down? Did he stay in Goliad and rest? No. Even though he knew he would die, he returned to the Alamo to bring the news he had been ordered to bring. On March 6, when all the defenders inside the Alamo were killed, he was among them. He gave his life willingly because he wanted to stand for separation and independence from Mexico.

God has called us as Christians to live differently from non-Christians. He has called us to separate ourselves from the ways of the secular world no matter what the cost. We've been called to separate ourselves from sin, and we'll need courage to stand firm because Satan will besiege us.

> Finally, be strong in the Lord and in his mighty power. Put on the full armor of God so that you can take your stand against the devil's schemes. For our struggle is not against flesh and blood, but against the rulers, against the authorities, against the powers of

this dark world and against the spiritual forces of
evil in the heavenly realms.

Ephesians 6:10-12

We all face temptation, and it takes a great deal of courage to
stand for God. It takes a great deal of courage to say *no* to this fallen
world's beliefs and values. Faced with the temptations to experiment
with drugs and premarital sex, our Christian teenagers can, in the power
of Jesus Christ, courageously say *no* despite tremendous peer pressure.
What's true of our teenagers is true of us adults. We need to say *no* to
"the lust of the flesh, the lust of the eyes, and the pride of life" (1 John
2:16, *The New King James Version*). We need to say *no* to lifestyles that
are centered on materialism, hedonism, and self-glorification. Although
it is not easy, we need to have deep, courageous commitment.

Since Christ's death, resurrection, and ascension, Christians
have never had easy lives. In 81 A.D., Emperor Domitian began ruling
the Roman Empire. Hideous and cruel, he ruled autocratically for
fifteen years and greatly persecuted Christians throughout the Roman
world. He also established what became known as the cult of Caesar,
which really amounted to Caesar worship. Throughout the Roman
world each year, the people had to burn incense on the altar of the
emperor in Roman temples. They also had to say three simple words:
"Caesar is lord." Then the worshippers received certificates of
compliance.

Even though they had been commanded to worship Caesar,
most Christians refused to comply. On penalty of death, they
courageously refused to say those three words. Historians reveal that
the Christians said, "Jesus is Lord," instead. Consequently, those
Christians were whipped, beaten, imprisoned, and even executed
because they would not deny Jesus Christ.

That's the kind of courage Jesus Christ is looking for today.
Everyday we are tempted to say, "Caesar is lord." Everyday we are
tempted to sin. Everyday we are tempted to leave the path God has set

146

for us. And everyday—every hour of the day—God wants us to say, "Jesus is Lord," and recommit our lives to Him. He is looking for courageous Christians who will serve Him faithfully.

If we have courage, God can use us, through the power of the Holy Spirit, to transform the world. If we have courage, He can keep the world from transforming us into its mold. We can be molded by Him and by Him alone.

Humility

CHAPTER FIFTEEN

The story is told of three passengers who were flying in a twin-engine airplane during a winter storm. One passenger was a computer programmer, another was a minister, and the third was a boy scout. As they flew, the left engine quit and could not be restarted. With ice accumulating on the wings, the airplane lost altitude.

Suddenly, the pilot appeared. "I've put the plane on autopilot, but it's going to crash soon," he stated. "There are no places nearby where we can land. We have only three parachutes on board. I shouldn't do this; but since I have a wife and three children, I'm leaving." He grabbed a parachute pack and jumped out the side door.

As the wind whipped through the airplane, the computer programmer looked at the minister and the boy scout. "I am probably the smartest man on earth," he said. "The world needs me. What I do, I do for all mankind." He also grabbed a pack and jumped out.

The minister thought for a moment, looked compassionately at the boy scout, and then said, "You are young. I've lived a long life, so it's only right that you take the last parachute. I'll go down with the plane."

"Relax, Reverend," the boy scout replied. "The world's smartest man just grabbed my rucksack and jumped."

The Bible tells us that those who exalt themselves will be humbled; and, certainly, that is what happened to the computer programmer. When we read Scripture, it's clear that this quality of humility is extremely precious to God. Yet for most of us humility remains an illusive goal, a concept difficult to define. We notice the actions of certain people and know with certainty that they don't have it. We look at other people and suspect that they are humble. We are afraid to think of ourselves as being humble for fear that the mere thought might remove us from the ranks of humble people.

Humility Means Lowering Ourselves

What is humility? What is it according to the Bible? Biblical humility can be defined in two ways. First, it means "to lower oneself." A humble person is willing to lower himself or herself in order to fulfill a godly purpose. The Greek word *tapeinos,* translated humility in the Bible, literally means "low." The Greeks didn't use it to describe a person who had low self-esteem or a poor self-image. Rather they used it to describe a person who was willing to lower himself or herself in order to promote the good of other people.

Our Lord Jesus Christ is the primary example of someone who lowered Himself. Before time began, He existed in the form of God. He was in the beginning with God. As the Son of God, He shared the very nature of God. Enthroned in glory, He was surrounded by myriads and myriads of angelic hosts who worshipped Him as King of kings and Lord of lords. He ruled the cosmos. Yet as the Bible records, in humility He lowered Himself. He was born in the likeness of man into our world, and He emptied Himself of His godly rights. For thirty-three years he shared our human form. As Paul described it,

> [Jesus] Who, being in the very nature God, did not
> consider equality with God something to be grasped,
> but made himself nothing, taking the very nature of
> a servant, being made in human likeness. And being

found in appearance as a man, he humbled himself
and became obedient to death — even death on a
cross!

Philippians 2:6-8

How did Paul introduce this wonderful passage? He wrote,
"Your attitude should be the same as that of Christ Jesus" (Philippians
2:5). God wants us to be humble. He wants us to be willing to lower
ourselves.

According to the Bible, there are only two mindsets: the mind of
Christ, who was willing to lower Himself; and the mind of Satan, who
only seeks to exalt himself. At the dawn of time, Satan, in fact, said in
his heart,

I will ascend to heaven; I will raise my throne above
the stars of God; I will sit enthroned on the mount of
assembly, on the utmost heights of the sacred
mountain. I will ascend above the tops of the clouds;
I will make myself like the Most High.

Isaiah 14:13-14

The Bible tells us that this world has adopted the mind of Satan,
not the mind of Christ. So many people want to exalt themselves. In fact,
if we're totally honest, most of us have to admit that from the moment
we came out of the womb we have been taught to exalt ourselves — to
make something of ourselves and to climb the ladder of success. The
economic system of capitalism and free enterprise is predicated on the
belief that people want to exalt themselves. Even the so-called Protestant
work ethic, in its basest form, promotes self-exaltation. When we look
back through history, we see that since the sin of Adam and Eve people
have always exalted themselves. Alexander the Great, Julius Caesar,
Genghis Khan, Napoleon Bonaparte, Adolph Hitler, and countless other
well-known and unknown people have sought to exalt themselves.

Some of them even sought to conquer and to rule the world.

Most of us today are not as proud as Alexander the Great or Julius Caesar, and we deal with much smaller portions of the world. But even in our small portions, we tend to seek to exalt ourselves and to demonstrate the mind of Satan.

Someone may be thinking, *Doesn't God want me to be productive, to bear fruit? Can I be productive and still have the mind of Christ by lowering myself?* Of course! God wants you to cultivate and to use your gifts, abilities, and aptitudes, but not in ways that exalt yourself. In fact, God says that in order to please Him you must be humble; you must be willing to lower yourself.

A paradox commonly pops up, however, when the subject of lowering ourselves arises. When we do lower ourselves, Satan encourages us to become proud of our "lowering!"

Dr. Harry Ironside, whom many in his generation considered to be the greatest preacher in America, received many accolades and much praise. Unfortunately, according to some historians, he believed most of them. According to one source, the following conversation occurred between Ironside and his wife.

> "You know, Harry," his wife remarked, "you need a little bit of humility."

> "I know that's true," he replied, "and I struggle with that. But I don't know how to become more humble."

> "I think you need to be humiliated," his wife responded. "I mean, I think it'd be good for you to be taken down a notch."

> 'What are you suggesting?" Ironside asked.

> "Well," she said, "I think you ought to get one of those

sandwich boards, put it over your head, and put the plan of salvation on the front board and the back board. Write 'all have sinned' and then 'repent.' Write, 'Believe in the Lord Jesus Christ and you will be saved.' Put John 3:16 and a few other passages on there, too.

"Then," she continued, "go to downtown Chicago, put on the sandwich board, and walk all day in the business district."

"I can't do that," Ironside stated. "I'm a respected preacher."

"That's just the point," she replied. "I think it'd be good for you."

According to the story, Ironside went downtown and walked the streets, wearing a sandwich board that announced, "Jesus Saves." All day long people mocked and ridiculed him, but he stayed. Then he returned home, removed the sandwich board, and sat down to reflect.

"Harry, what are you thinking?" his wife asked.

"Well," he said, "I was thinking that there's not another minister in America who would have been willing to do what I did today."

Have you noticed that the moment we each do something that is lowly we have the tendency to feel proud of what we have done? It's as if we lower ourselves in order to exalt ourselves. Satan works in such subtle ways, and the meaning of humility can seem elusive. Perhaps that's why the Bible gives us a second definition of humility.

Humility Means Exalting Others

According to Scripture, humility doesn't simply mean "the lowering of self." It also means "to exalt others." In fact, God calls us to lower ourselves for the purpose of exalting other people. If we are to be humble, we must lower ourselves in order to exalt the Lord and other people for His sake.

Again, Jesus Christ is our example. He lowered Himself in order to exalt His Father. He lowered Himself in order to exalt all mankind. He came to earth and died on the cross so that we, as a result of our personal faith in Him, might live in eternity with Him. He allowed His body to be broken in order that we might become spiritually whole. He lowered Himself so that we might be exalted. Likewise, He wants us to lower ourselves willingly for His name's sake and for the sake of His kingdom.

In Great Britain a few centuries ago, the English people commonly hunted and ate wild deer. The kings and their courts loved venison and ate the better cuts of deer meat, such as roasts and steaks. The servants and the huntsmen, on the other hand, ate the more lowly, leftover portions called the "umbles"—the heart, the liver, and the gizzard. Often these lowly portions were made into a pie, which in a play on words became known as umble pie.

But the servants and the huntsmen were not demonstrating humility when they ate the umbles. No doubt they would have preferred to eat steaks and roasts, too. They, however, didn't have a choice. They were forced to eat the lowly portions so that the kings and their courts could eat the better portions.

If you and I really want to be humble, we must freely choose to lower ourselves and to exalt other people. We must choose to eat umble pie. We must choose lowly portions so that other people may receive the better portions and be exalted. That's difficult to do in our society, isn't it? It's contrary to how most people think. In fact, it's totally contrary to the way in which most of us have been taught to think and how deep down inside we want to think.

Martin Luther, referred to by some as the Father of Protestantism, was a brilliant leader and courageous man of God. The principal leader of the Protestant Reformation, he courageously nailed the *Ninety-Five Theses* to the door of the Wittenberg Castle Church in Wittenberg, Germany. It was Luther who defied papal authority and renounced the indulgences and the abuses of the Roman Catholic Church. It was Luther who elevated Scripture and the authority of Scripture above the authority of the Roman Catholic Church. It was Luther who emphatically taught that salvation and justification can be received only by grace through faith. It was Luther who translated the Latin and the Greek Bible into German, thus shaping the modern German language and, more importantly, making the Bible available to common, everyday people.

But was Luther able to accomplish all this by himself? No. Have you heard of Philipp Melanchthon? Like Luther, Melanchthon had been a professor at the University of Wittenberg. Considered by some historians to be the Teacher of Germany because of his influence on Germany's high school and university education, Melanchthon was the greatest New Testament Greek scholar in Europe. Yet Christ used him to exalt Luther.

You see, Philipp Melanchthon helped Martin Luther translate the Bible into beautiful German, but Luther received all the praise. Melanchthon was the principal author of the Augsburg Confession, the leading confessional statement of the Lutheran Church today. When Luther needed practical help and wisdom concerning matters of theology, piety, ecclesiology, exegesis, and hermeneutics, Melanchthon availed himself and was glad to work behind the scenes, lowering himself so that Luther might be exalted. Thus, in addition to being Luther's best friend, Melanchthon played a key role in shaping much of Luther's life and thought.

When Martin Luther died in 1546, Philipp Melanchthon gave the sermon at the funeral and the committal over his friend's grave. When Melanchthon died, his body was lowered into that same grave! Today they rest side by side on the property of Wittenberg Castle Church, equal in death even though they were never equal in the eyes of the world.

When Luther and Melanchthon stand before the judgment seat of Christ, as we all must, which of them will receive the greater reward? Both of them "fought the good fight." Both of them "finished the race." Both of them "kept the faith." (See 2 Timothy 4:7.) I'm sure that Christ will say to both of them, in effect, "Come, O blessed of My Father. Inherit the kingdom prepared for you from before the foundation of the world." Yet I can't help but wonder if God will give Melanchthon a special reward for his humility.

Speaking of the world to come, Jesus Himself said, "many who are first will be last, and many who are last will be first" (Matthew 19:30). Truly, those people who exalt themselves will be humbled, and those people who humble themselves will be exalted (Matthew 23:12).

Praise God for individuals who are willing to labor behind the scenes for the cause of Christ, who are lowering themselves so that others might be exalted. Praise God for people who desire to be faithful to God's calling and who are not seeking their own glory.

The apostle John recorded a wonderful scene that we should keep in mind. During the evening, before serving the Last Supper, Jesus got up from the meal and wrapped a towel around His waist. He poured water into a basin and washed each of His disciples' dirty feet, using the towel to dry them. Afterward Jesus returned to His place at the table.

> 'Do you understand what I have done for you?' he asked them. 'You call me "Teacher" and "Lord," and rightly so, for that is what I am. Now that I, your Lord and Teacher, have washed your feet, you also should wash one another's feet. I have set you an example that you should do as I have done for you.'
>
> John 13:12-15